ENDORSEMENTS FOR GARDEN WISD

Cheryl Wilfong shows us how to cultivate the inner garden with lovely, often funny, and always wise stories and reflections. The more I read, the happier I got!
> —RICK HANSON, PhD; author, *Buddha's Brain: The Practical Neuroscience of Happiness, Love, and Wisdom*

Cheryl's newest book tells you how to journey from the garden to the Garden by way of mindfulness.
> —SHINZEN YOUNG; author, *The Science of Enlightenment*

Discover with fresh eyes the beauty and perfection all around us and the goodness and wisdom right inside us. A beautiful book in every way!
> —JAMES BARAZ; founding teacher, Spirit Rock Meditation Center; author, *Awakening Joy*

Nature and mindfulness are a a hand and glove fit.
> —JUDSON BREWER, MD, PhD; Director of Research, Center for Mindfulness; Associate Professor, Medicine and Psychiatry, University of Massachusetts Medical School; Adjunct Assistant Professor, Yale School of Medicine; Research Affiliate, Department of Brain and Cognitive Sciences, MIT

Fresh and fun and insightful.
> —JAN FRAZIER; author, *When Fear Falls Away: The Story of A Sudden Awakening* and *The Freedom of Being: At Ease With What Is*

Grow the wisdom of your heart with these inspiring daily reminders of mindfulness.
> —LEIGH BRASINGTON; author, *Right Concentration: A Practical Guide to the Jhanas*

TO Nancy,
May your garden flourish!
Love,
Cheryl

GARDEN WISDOM
365 DAYS

Cheryl Wilfong

Cheryl Wilfong
Heart Path Press, L3C
314 Partridge Road
Putney VT 05346

www.meditativegardener.com

Garden Wisdom: 365 Days

BOOK DESIGN BY CAROLYN KASPER

ISBN: 978-0-9972729-4-9

cover photo and page i credit: tolgaildun / iStock; page iii and v photo credit: shutterstock;
page vii photo credit: MementoImage / iStock; all others as indicated

Dedicated to Elisha DiMatteo,
who makes my garden—and my writing about
the garden—possible.

ALSO BY CHERYL WILFONG

CONTENTS

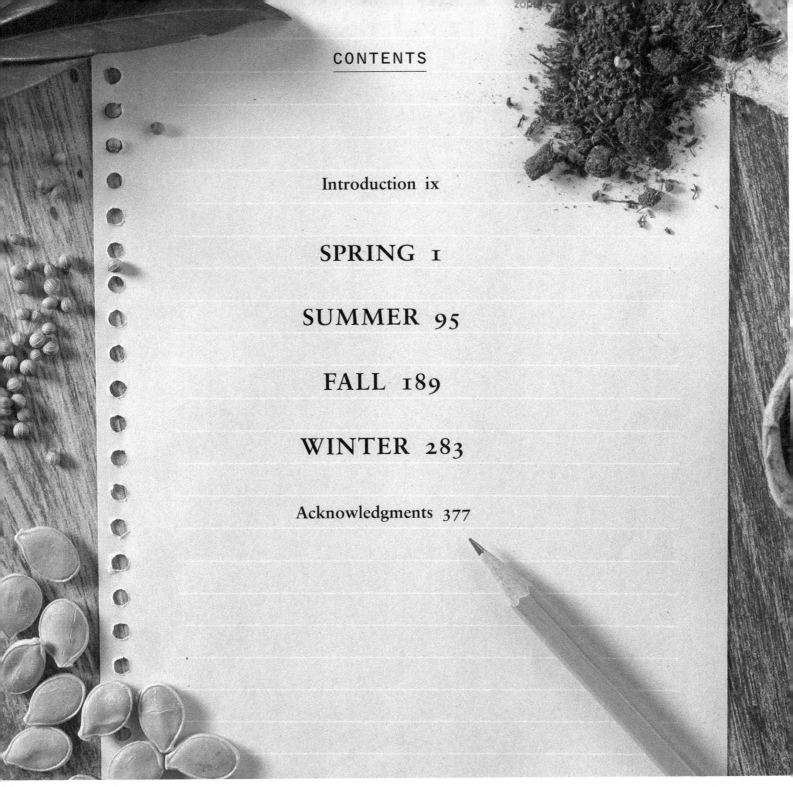

INTRODUCTION

Since publishing my award-winning book *The Meditative Gardener: Cultivating Mindfulness of Body, Feelings, and Mind* a few years ago, I've written an almost-daily blog about taking our mindfulness practice out to the garden. The obvious parallels between nature and human nature are endlessly fascinating. The wisdom of life can be found in our very own garden—whether that means a flower pot on the front step, a vegetable garden in the backyard, or, in my case, 32 different gardens.

I love gardening: I'm a Master Gardener and a Master Composter. And I love mindfulness: I teach meditation at Vermont Insight Meditation Center. I also enjoy writing: my blog www.TheMeditativeGardener.blogspot.com has won a Blogisattva Award and is one of 52 Meditation Blogs You Have to Read in 2017.

In *Garden Wisdom 365 Days* you can read the best of the blog, and take your mindfulness multi-vitamin every day.

SPRING

GREETING SPRING IN THE GARDEN

My sweetie gave me a garden sign for Christmas:

> *I love spring anywhere,*
> *but if I could choose*
> *I would always greet it in a garden.*

I love these lines from Ruth Stout, the celebrated garden writer, who gardened and wrote into her nineties.

I am greeting spring snow here in my garden, where it is hard to imagine that in six weeks, I'll be hosting a garden party. Flowers will be blooming, and bees will be buzzing. A revolution is about to happen—in weather and in the flowerbeds—but at the moment, all is quiet.

We sit quietly in meditation (whether or not our mind is quiet). Today's meditation seems pretty much the same as yesterday's. We can't imagine anything different, really. And then, when we least expect it, a revolution happens—an insight. We see something differently. Sometimes an insight can change our lives.

So we sit—watching the fluffy snow. Do we notice how it melts into rivulets, or consider the spring-rushing brook that is about to wash us clean?

COMPARING SNOW

All sorts of grumbling are occurring around here about *the snow*. Harrumph. It's supposed to be spring.

Our Facebook friends in California are posting pictures of magnolia blossoms, and all we have to look at are the pregnant buds of the red maple.

It's cold here. And the snowplow can't plow because the dirt roads are muddy underneath the snow. Bah, humbug.

Can you hear the comparing mind at work? "It's supposed to be" spring, but it looks like winter. Flowers are blooming elsewhere, but not here. It's cold here (18 degrees this morning). It was warm last week when I was in Cancun/Costa Rica/the Caribbean/Tel Aviv.

The mind compares our present experience with some other past or imaginary experience, and then we feel dissatisfied with the present moment.

We could simply experience the raw data of the present moment: chilly, sunny, snowy, beautiful, hungry birds, red maple buds. This is the truth of the moment—before our opinions reclaim our attention and twist our hearts into grumpiness.

SNOWDROPS IN THE SNOW

Snowdrops are blooming—in the snow, of course. Despite 16-degree mornings and breezy, chilly (though sunny) afternoons, this little flower breaks through winter's dying crust and flowers now.

Even in our coldest times, we may see a sprig of green. A friend called for help yesterday. Her 33-year-old son is paranoid and depressed, and she is 3,200 miles away.

Perhaps you have lived through such a bleak time, as I have too. In the dark night of the psyche, such as when a relationship has withered and died, it's hard to believe that the sun will ever shine again. This is when I first began meditating. Sometimes the calm, the relief from severe anxiety, would last for five minutes. Sometimes it would last for five hours.

The cold winds blow. A tiny white flower blooms.

photo credit: shutterstock

SPRING OF SPRINGS

Spring has sprung, and around here, springs are gushing. Many of these rivulets that begin as underground springs form seasonal streams—rills—that dry up in April and don't start running again until mud season next March.

These dancing, energetic, watery children grow into swift-flowing creeks, and run on into slower rivers. Streams around my home flow into Salmon Brook, so named for the famed Atlantic salmon; sadly, however, the brook hasn't seen any salmon in a couple of hundred years.

Salmon can taste their home water, and so return there to spawn and die.

We too can know "home," as we "taste" calmness, joy, love, and compassion. When we begin to recognize these tastes, we can head straight home by sitting down to meditate.

SUN SHED

I bought the cutest garden shed about ten years ago. It has windows on the south side, so I thought I could use it as a greenhouse. Oh, the lure of a greenhouse!

As it turns out, March nights are freezing in the little sunshed, and April days are sweltering. The plants perish if I forget to water them every forenoon and every afternoon. So, the sun shed has become a storage shed with a lot of south-facing windows.

Desire does funny things to our minds and feelings. The garden shed is still cute, but all those windows enable passers-by to look in and see all the junk stored there. Piles of flower pots and stacks of garden stakes are not very scenic.

How many, many things we buy that don't quite live up to our dreams and expectations. I now buy things knowing that my probability of giving them away is higher than my probability of keeping them. I try to watch the feeling of desire rising in my body, and remember the tricks that desire plays with my mind.

I think about giving away the sun shed or selling it at half price. But then, where would I store my gardening paraphernalia?

COLTSFOOT & DANDELION

The first spring wildflower is blooming along the edges of dirt roads near marshy areas. At first, I thought it was a dandelion, but its bright yellow flowers have no leaves when they blossom.

Coltsfoot is named for the shape of its leaf, just as dandelion or "dent de lion" (lion's tooth) is named for its leaf shape. The leaves of both plants make tasty early-spring salads.

Gardeners may consider coltsfoot and dandelion invasive "weeds," but herbalists use coltsfoot leaves to treat colds, flu, and asthma. The dandelion, too, is completely useful—its flowers for cosmetics, its leaves to provide Vitamins A and C, and its root as a coffee substitute or as a magenta dye.

Isn't it interesting how our "enemies"—plants, in this case—turn out to befriend us when we look at them more deeply?

photo credit: shutterstock

RAKING THE DRIVEWAY

I was so desperate to do something outdoors yesterday that I raked the driveway.

Since I live in the woods, a winter's worth of sticks, pine needles, and pine cones has accumulated along the edges. These informal "gutters" need to be kept clear of debris so that the melt water and spring rain water can flow freely downhill and not "pond" or become diverted into the garage.

Our minds also accumulate debris every day, as our attention is diverted from mindfulness of the flow of life. Instead, stress runs into the house of the ego. "But what about me?" churns in the mind.

Rake your attention toward the underlying feelings of bother or anticipation or just plain don't-know-ness. Soak in the discomfort, the un-ease. And notice that life continues to flow.

BLOOMING BROMELIAD

My bromeliad is blooming! Although pineapple is the most familiar member of this family, hundreds of bromeliads grow in the tropics, and some few of those have become our houseplants.

My bromeliad came from a friend who was suffering severe respiratory problems and off-loading all her houseplants because she was allergic to the molds and mildews in the potting soil.

When our distress becomes great enough, we simplify our lives and give away our sources of suffering. At one time, we thought such things were beautiful or desirable, and our friends may still think so. But our viewpoint has changed, and we see things as they really are.

This is one step on our path to awakening.

photo credit: Namepic / iStock

PLANTING HYACINTH BULBS

The hyacinths that I started forcing on November 15 began blooming on January 17. The bulbs now sit in their vases of water, looking extremely aged and ugly.

It's the time to plant them in a flowerbed. Last year's hyacinths are blooming in the garden now, and I am happy to see them. Hyacinths seem to decline over three or four years, with fewer flowers on their stalks every year, so I enjoy this opportunity to replenish them.

Planting the bulbs now means that I can put them exactly where I want them, whereas in the fall, when bulb planting is like playing blind man's bluff. "Let's see. Where were those daffodils? Where were those Siberian squill? Hmmm. Where exactly do I want to plant hyacinths?"

How can we create similarly favorable conditions for our meditation practice to bloom? Going on retreat is one way to jump-start our practice. Then we can plant ourselves on the cushion at home with more intention. Perhaps we can find a nearby meditation group where we can sit weekly with others while also sprouting some spiritual friendships.

May kindness and calmness bloom in your heart.

MICRO-CLIMATES

Now—during the change of seasons—is a good time to notice the micro-climates in your garden.

Yesterday, the first two crocuses bloomed at the southeast corner of my house, where it is both sunny and well protected from the prevailing northwesterly winds. The hillside on the east side of my house is always the first to lose the snow; it's not only well protected, it slopes at an angle that's good for catching the sun's rays. (Think of the angle of greenhouse windows, for example.)

I've been toying with the idea of a cold frame, and that warm, sun-collecting place, protected (by the house) from spring's northwest winds seems like a perfect and easily accessible place.

What's the micro-climate you need for your meditation? Quiet? Warm? Cool? (A warm room puts me to sleep.) Outdoors? Indoors? Early? Late? Mid-afternoon?

Find the time and the place in your home where the conditions are just right for growing your meditation practice.

THE SNOWPLOW DOES SOME GARDENING FOR ME

Living here in the North Country means having to plow your driveway after every snowfall.

Herein comes the dilemma: the snowplow or the garden?

To defend my kitchen garden, at the end of the driveway, from the winter's moraine of driveway gravel, I installed two sections of fence separated by an arbor—a lovely transition from the parking area to a green and flowering "room" during spring, summer, and fall.

The male in my household comes down firmly on the side of the snowplow, and faithfully removes the fencing every November. In April, after snowmelt, I may have to remind him to replace the walls of my herb garden "room."

Every spring, I find that the snowplow has done some gardening for me. Three years ago, I found a green-and-white hosta growing in the woods. How did it get there?

It took me a while to piece together the story of the snowplow nicking it out of the side of the driveway and bulldozing it into the huge snow fort at the end of his run. The hosta survived. As did a delicate lady fern the following year.

This spring I found mitella (miterwort) and White Nancy lamium, refugees from my white garden at the front door, camped about 20 feet away in a grove of maidenhair fern.

Of course, the question is not *either* the snowplow *or* the garden.

The answer is: the snowplow *and* the garden.

POPPY SEED SNOW

"It's snowing!" my dad would say at 6:30 A.M. every April 1. My eyes would pop open, and I'd jump out of bed and run to the window.

"April Fool's!" he'd grin.

Today in the North Country, it *is* snowing, and it is April Fool's. This may (or may not) be our last snow of the year, our poor (wo)man's fertilizer. Today is the day to plant poppies by throwing poppy seeds on top of the snow.

I particularly like *Papaver somniflorum* (sleep flower), the opium poppy, which is a re-seeding annual. I'll be planting other cold-happy seeds as well, such as larkspur. Any later than this, and the results, i.e., the plants, become a bit iffy because these seeds require cool weather to germinate.

During cold internal weather, when you feel the world has snowed you in—this is the time to start meditating. Close your eyes for a moment. Plant mindfulness today.

Although the immediate forecast may seem bleak, remember: some seeds germinate more successfully in the cold. I'm strapping on my snowshoes right now and going out to the garden to mindfully sow poppy seeds.

BEAUTY AND WISDOM

The flowerbeds are popping. All of a sudden, flowers are blooming—yellow crocus, little purple iris reticulata, and white-belled leucojum. Morning temperatures still hover in the twenties, so the bloomers seem to be hugging the ground for warmth. Even leucojum (summer snowflake), which is generally 16 inches tall, is blooming at four inches.

"Youth is wasted on the young," they say. Youth is beautiful and naive and takes health and wealth (e.g., an allowance) for granted.

Our young gardens are beginning to bloom into heart-opening beauty. Perhaps we take the health and bounty of our flowerbeds for granted in this season as we begin to dream of a lush summer garden.

Wisdom and equanimity allow us to enjoy beauty while also seeing that the beauty of our physical bodies, like the beauty of our flower gardens, will age and die. How could it be otherwise?

We may be old ourselves, but we can bloom with wisdom.

photo credit: shutterstock

THE PERSON I USED TO BE

April showers have come early this year, and the creeks are running near flood stage. Spring run-off, we say. And where does the spring of our life run off to? Where is that young face and lithe body?

The photos of the person I call "me" delude me into thinking that's the person I am. That person in the picture, that Cheryl, is dead now.

Yes, I can remember her—sort of. Five years of college, living with her boyfriend in Florida. She was a VISTA[1] volunteer in Utah, and I can tell you about all those national parks on the Colorado River Plateau. She fell in love with a Japanese-American and followed him to Hawai'i. She then moved to Vermont to earn a Master's degree.

I live here still.

The events of that young woman's life set in motion a wave, whose ripples I still feel today.

The creek is roaring outside the window. In summer, it becomes calm and tinkling. Now, in the autumn of my life, the mindstream is littered with the fallen leaves of memories—some clogging little channels, and some settling to the bottom to decompose.

The creek flows on. A young middle-aged old life runs its course, never able to flow backwards to the person I used to be.

---

1 VISTA is the acronym for Volunteers In Service To America

BLOODROOT

Bloodroot is blooming, its simple white flower tucked in the cloak of a single grape-like leaf, as if it has turned up its collar against the winter wind. This ephemeral wildflower grows in little colonies—but not where I originally planted it.

Right now, it's blossoming in the middle of a triangular flowerbed—right where I've planted all the tall summer-blooming plants. But the tall perennials haven't peeked their heads out of the winter bed yet, so the tiny bloodroot may as well flower there at center stage. Another bloodroot is blooming between two stones in the walk near the front door.

Never mind that I can't control bloodroot. I simply put it in a place where I thought it would look good, and now it grows of its own accord.

We also plant wholesome thoughts and actions in our everyday lives. And then one day, we notice, "Oh, I used to be mad at this person. And now I'm not." Or, "Oh, this situation used to make me anxious. And right now, it doesn't."

That's the benefit of sowing the seeds of skillful actions. You never know where they will show up.

COOL CYCLAMENS

I'm setting my cyclamens outdoors beside the front door, because they like it cool.

On a theater tour to London one January, I was amazed at the number of cyclamens in window boxes. Beautiful! Cyclamens can withstand a bit of snow and frost. They wilt in the heat and go dormant in the summer.

When meditating, my mind is more alert when my body is cool, even on the verge of goose bumps, because warmth wilts my meditation. Therefore, I almost never wear my beautiful purple meditation shawl from Nepal. I take off my sweater and my scarf (if I'm wearing one). Most importantly, I take off my socks. Socks = sleepiness.

Finding the right temperature for our meditation can be a matter of fine-tuning. While I was on a month-long retreat, I noticed that the woman who sat next to me wore three blankets, a hat, a neck scarf, mittens, and toasty slippers; she also had a blanket over her feet. I sat barefoot in the 62-degree meditation hall.

A shivering cyclamen really appeals to me, because it reminds me to stay cool during meditation. Each person's and each flower's thermostat is different. This refrigerator weather "saves" the early blooms, and yet the warm afternoons entice the mid-season bloomers. At what temperature does your meditation bloom?

AMARYLLIS PATIENCE

An amaryllis is blooming in my solarium. I bought this pot of two bulbs at a library plant sale. I've been watering their strappy green leaves for almost two years, and finally—flowers!

Sometimes we feel that nothing is happening, even though we consistently water our meditation practice.

Patience, my dear friend. Patience with your meditation. Patience with your nearest and dearest. Patience with your aging parents and with your co-workers.

Patience is one of the ten supreme qualities that we practice, practice, practice. After all, practice makes perfect.

Patience is an antidote to irritation. "Count to ten," your mother said. Nowadays, you might count ten breaths before you respond.

Patience is an antidote to desire. Watch desire arise in the mind. Feel "I want" in your body. Notice that it passes. Even if the same desire re-posts itself in your mind one-half second later.

Patience is an antidote to confusion. You don't actually need to know the answer to the question right this minute (although you may want the answer right now). Feel confusion in your body. Watch the ripples of confusion in your mind. Patience is a remedy that cures many ills, many dis-eases of the mind.

Patience, my dear. It has taken the amaryllis two years to bloom.

APRIL IS THE CRUELEST MONTH

"April is the cruelest month," said T. S. Eliot. Such disappointment is one form of stress and distress.

Today: seventy degrees, flowers blooming, birds singing—what's not to love? Falling in love with Spring feels great!

Year after year, I forget how fickle April is. Just after I've skimmed down to shorts and a tank top, April turns a cold shoulder, and I must cover myself in fleece. Just when my face is tanning from the warm sun, my lover April pelts me with cold showers. Just when my body relaxes into April's embrace, she chills out, and I shiver.

Oh April! Receiver of my pent-up passion for gardening.

When hopes and dreams and expectations are dashed, dissatisfaction weighs down our hearts, and we call it cruel.

photo credit: shutterstock

PANSY SUBSTITUTES

I love pansies. Their cheerful faces reflect the way I feel now that spring is springing. But given the vast stretches of tan-brown in my flowerbeds, a six-pack of pansies doesn't go very far. That's the reason I now put these multi-color delights in a big pot right beside the door. I can see them and smile every time I come home. A container of pansies looks full and inviting.

Out in the vegetable garden, Johnny-jump-ups are beginning to bloom. There are so many that I treat them like weeds. But now I realize I can transplant my bumper crop of Johnny-jump-ups into flowerbeds near the house and have the thrill of pansies. they have the same sweet smiling faces—just smaller.

Sometimes, the happiness or calm we hoped to gain from meditation just isn't as full as we expected it to be. Life can look rather brown and dingy. Look closely at the sweetness/joy/contentment that you *do* experience in meditation. It may be very small. In fact, it may be very, very small—just one second. Transplant that one second into your life repeatedly, and pretty soon you'll have a whole pot full of happiness every time you come home to meditation.

SPROUTING MINDFULNESS

My neighbor Connie has started arugula and spinach in a three-foot-square patch of...well, lawn, actually. On the south side of her deck, she cleared a bit of grass, sowed her seeds at the end of March, and covered them with clear plastic. The plastic both retains moisture and warms the earth, since we are still in maple sugaring season here (when nights are below freezing and days are above).

One-half-inch-tall green sprouts (hardy!) are growing in short rows, so she has rolled the plastic back. Now that the plants have gotten started, they can withstand the chill of the nights.

We can start our meditation practice anywhere: in the car, washing dishes, going to the bathroom. All we need is the intention to take a mindful moment.

Choose one daily activity to be mindful of: walking down a familiar hallway, waiting at a stoplight, listening to the phone ringing two times before answering on the third ring.

Roll back the plastic busy-ness that covers your life and notice the sprouts of mindfulness.

HAPPIFYING TULIPS

I started tulips in pots before Thanksgiving and put them in the garage for their winter vacation—not exactly dark, but dim and above freezing I brought them indoors in mid-February, and it took longer than I expected for them to bloom.

One early April, when I came home from three weeks of retreat, my sweetie had set ten pots of blooming tulips on the front step. Outdoors, they last for two or three weeks, in the refrigerator weather of early spring, while indoors, in the warmth, they come and go in less than a week.

I love the tulip blast on the front step. Not much is blooming in the gardens just yet, so all those tulips are not only colorful but happifying as well.

What leads to your happiness? Flowers? Birds? Nature? A walk in the woods? Happiness opens the heart and relaxes the mind. We need five times as much happiness to balance the negativity that is all around us, beginning in our minds with little bothers and nuisances, frustrations and impatience.

Include some happiness in your day today.

LOOK-ALIKES AND FEEL-ALIKES

The tree service came and cut down three black birch trees. Black birches look very much like cherry trees. To tell them apart, break a twig. If it's black birch, the scent of wintergreen washes over you. Chew on the little stick, and refresh your breath. I now have a pile of wood chips that smells like a wintergreen LifeSaver factory. Ahhh.

I use these wood chips for my garden paths. After hauling a dozen garden-cartloads, I simply lie down on the brand-new wood-chip path and inhale that wonderful aroma.

The sublime emotions that we cultivate in meditation—loving-kindness, compassion, appreciative joy—each have a "near enemy"—a worldly emotion that looks and feels very similar to the sublime emotion, but just doesn't "smell" as wonderful.

For instance, the near enemy of compassion is pity. "Oh, those poor people." Pity closes off a little corner of the heart. "There but for the grace of God go I." Whew! I escaped that terrible thing. "My heart goes out to them" (but how about allowing them right into your heart?)

Compassion opens the heart wide—no holds and no bars—because when we look closely, we can find that other person in ourselves.

The "flavor" of compassion is different from that of pity. The flavor of loving-kindness is different from that of attachment. The flavor of appreciative joy is different than from that of the comparing mind that checks to see whether we have more or less, or even the same, as others.

Relax into compassion or loving-kindness today, and breathe in their wonderful fragrances.

MANNA IN THE GARDEN

Ten yards of mulch was just delivered. Every year, in mid-April, I order a special "Manna Mix," which is half compost and half mulch.

Manna, which fell from heaven, fed the wandering Israelites in the desert for forty years[2]. More prosaically, this manna mix feeds my flowerbeds, which in turn delight my eyes and pleasure my mind.

What feeds us spiritually? A bit of quiet time? A moment of solitude? A stroll through our gardens? Bringing mindfulness to this moment relaxes the body and relaxes the chattering mind.

When we let down our guard, as we can safely do in the garden, we can relax into our authentic selves. We come home to ourselves and are sustained by the manna of our gardens.

---

2   Exodus 16:14–36

photo credit: James Pauls / iStock

SHORT-LIVED REDBUD

Several years ago, I brought home a gallon of redbud seeds from the woods near the house in which I grew up, in Indiana. Redbud (*Cercis canadensis*) is a delightful little spring-blooming tree, whose pinky-red "buds" are followed by heart-shaped leaves.

I now live on the northernmost edge of the redbud's range, so I planted my little seedlings in the sunniest location I have, at the edge of the woods, facing south. One of those redbuds now arches over a third of my herb garden, and soon the redbud will fall victim to the construction of a new garage.

Something dear and delightful is going to die—very soon. Everything we cherish will perish.

We could take the attitude "Eat, drink, and be merry, for tomorrow we die," but this intemperateness trades sadness for momentary pleasure.

Seeing clearly the loss we face, we could instead feel grateful for what we do have. Gratitude leads to joy, and joy feels like love.

I love my redbud tree.

MARRIED TO MY GARDENS

My sweetie accuses me of spending my libido on the garden in the spring. As much as I deny it, maybe he's not far wrong.

Now that I'm putting my hands in dirt most days, I've taken off my rings and won't put them on again until the end of gardening in November. You could say I'm married to my gardens.

At dawn, I jump out of bed at first birdsong and leave my bed partner snoozing while I go see what's new in the garden. These April evenings I spend with my seedlings, transplanting them into pots, leaving my sweetie alone.

It's true: in the spring, my passion goes into the garden. I spend more hours with my garden each day than I do with my sweetie.

But he, too, enjoys a passion—music. He spends more hours with his piano every day than I spend in meditation. He cannot go to bed without playing his grand piano for half an hour.

We could be jealous of one another, or we can be happy for the other person: he is doing something that fulfills him, and I am doing something different that fulfills me. Amid our busy lives, we meet and look into one another's eyes, deeply grateful for each other.

HEPATICA ARE BLOOMING

Hepatica are blooming in the woods. This early wildflower pokes its dime-size pastel-colored flowers out of a carpet of dead leaves to dance in the spring breeze, even while its liver-shaped leaves still huddle near the ground for what warmth there may be.

I have one little patch of hepatica in my ten acres. I have never seen any in my neighbors' surrounding 75 acres. *I have something you don't have. Nah-nah-nah nah-nah-nah.*

How we long to take credit for situations as if they belonged to us. How we love to bolster I/me/mine. But does the hepatica "belong" to me? It was there in the woods when I moved here 35 years ago, and with luck, it will probably be there when I die. Does that make it mine?

How we take pride in our bodies:

- *I didn't need reading glasses until I was 56.*
- *I weigh the same as I did in high school.*
- *When I bend over, my hands touch the floor.*

We say these things as if we controlled our bodies, but life doesn't work like that. Yes, we can set up favorable conditions—a good diet, exercise, preventive maintenance—but unexpected things happen, including aging. That's when we know that, really, we are *not* in control.

Meanwhile, hepatica are blooming in the woods, spring is happening, and we are alive in such bodies as we have.

"MY BODY CAN'T KEEP UP WITH MY MIND"

I went to pick up a truckload of manure from Charlie at Sweet Tree Farm recently. We talked about the beautiful weather, and about all the things we'd like to get done.

"My body can't keep up with my mind," he said. "Yesterday, I only got about half the things done that I wanted to."

He's right.

The mind drives the body incessantly. "Do this." "Go there." "Make this."

The body silently obeys until it simply cannot do or go anymore, and we collapse—in front of the TV or into bed. Or into old age.

Contemplate this relationship between mind and body the next time you are considering your "to-do" list.

I'll contemplate it while I'm spreading that truckload of manure in the garden. *If* my body can keep up with my mind.

GASPING GARDENS

The garden is gasping. Although we've had three sprinkles since the beginning of April, rainfall adds up to only one-tenth of an inch so far this month. In March, we had one-half inch of rain, and in February one. The soil feels like powder.

Fortunately, my well produces 12 gallons a minute, so I have begun watering the flowerbeds. And the beds have a new covering of mulch, which holds dampness in the soil (just in case there is any) and prevents evaporation.

As our bodies age, various lubricating fluids become scarcer. The post-menopausal woman is most aware of this. The first thing that happened to me was frozen shoulders, a classic symptom of the synovial fluid in the joints beginning to disappear. A year (for each side) of daily physical therapy exercises and yoga eventually restored mobility.

For now, the gardens are living on their store of energy and available moisture, and our bodies do the same. The garden looks the same as in a rainy spring, and I look less and less like I did in the springtime of my life.

Let's go get a drink of water and recognize that the water in the glass is no different from the water in the body is no different from the water in a daffodil.

EASTER BUNNY VISITS TODAY!

It's snowing! All the easier to track the Easter bunny.

The Easter bunny is visiting me this afternoon, several days early, with a *really* big present—a truckload of bunny manure. These little chocolate-colored balls are mild enough that they can be scattered right on the gardens; they don't burn plants, and the manure is weed-free.

Think about it: pellets in, pellets out. No weeds in the bunnies' dinner means no weed seeds, unlike other, larger animal manures.

This chain of cause and effect applies to our lives as well. Let's practice wise and skillful speech that is true, useful, and beneficial—both outwardly with other people (including in cyberspace) and inwardly, in our own thoughts. That way, we'll find we have fewer weeds of discontent and unhappiness growing in our minds.

When visitors to my garden look puzzled and say, "Hey. Isn't that bunny…?" I just nod and smile.

THE MOMENTARY FRAGRANCE OF EASTER LILIES

My sweetie plays the organ at church, and on Easter Sunday, he brought home an Easter lily. We have enjoyed its blooms all week, but the greatest pleasure is walking into the house at night. When the deep fragrance of Easter lily hits our nostrils, it smells like heaven.

As we well know, the sense of smell very quickly acclimates, and, after a minute or two, we no longer smell the wonderful scent.

Our other physical senses—taste, touch, seeing, and hearing—also acclimate. We fill up on one taste, and think we are full, but we then mysteriously have room for dessert (a different flavor). Often people who live near airports, highways, or busy intersections don't hear the noise anymore.

We tune out 95 percent of our experience, so we can pay attention to whatever is changing. Our sixth sense—the mind—stays extremely busy, leading us from one train of thought to another. Our mind is always "changing," and that's where our attention goes. Some of us "live" in our minds.

One definition of mindfulness is "keeping mind together with body." Bring the mind to the body sitting. Right now. Notice what your hands are doing. Pay attention to your feet. Notice reading and the movement of the eyes.

Notice life.

WILD LEEKS

Wild leeks are growing in the woods. Their roots look like scallions, but their two or three leaves are broad, like those of lily-of-the-valley. Also called ramps, the wild leeks definitely smell like onions. When you find them, you'll know it, as these wild leeks carpet the forest floor with greenery. The colony I found yesterday was 50 yards long and 15 yards wide.

Wild leeks grow in calcium-rich soils, which, while not rare around here, are not common either. Blue cohosh grows among the wild leeks, as do trillium and Dutchman's breeches. Nature's companion plants grow in the same habitat.

We plant ourselves among those who support us in nurturing our best traits. And we cross our fingers, hoping that our children and teens will likewise choose the "right" peer group. We know very well the consequences of hanging out with those of questionable moral character.

Do your companions nurture the best in you?

photo credit: shutterstock

BUGS—ON THE PLANTS AND IN THE BODY

The houseplants have been cooped up in the house all winter; now, with the change of season, they're getting bugs. And I've caught a bug too.

I set the sickest houseplants on the front step to sun themselves, enjoy a rainwater bath, and take in some fresh air. Their anti-bio-tic consists of the bigger bugs that will dine on the little aphids and spider mites. I myself am taking hot baths and bundling up to stay warm in order to balance the cold that's affecting my respiration.

We are of the nature to become ill. Sickness is unavoidable. I didn't ask to become ill. I don't want to be sick. Yet, here is the body, feeling poorly and fighting off some intruding bug. Sunning myself today, after a hot water bath, should ease the discomfort.

PLEASANT AND UNPLEASANT

Overcast skies. Misting rain and 46 degrees. The weather looks unpleasant, so I've avoided going out to the garden for as long as I can. I want to work in the garden, yet I don't want to go outdoors. Approach/avoidance.

I think about a project I want to do. This project sits in a line of dominoes: I want to order another truckload of bark mulch, but I have to clean up the load of wood chips that is sitting right where the truck will dump the mulch. In order to use the wood chips on a path around the moss garden, I have to widen the path first. This means I have to move the big rocks that border the path and reset them. Are we tired yet?

Finally, after repeatedly looking out the window at the project area, I find that desire (pleasant) trumps all those little unpleasantnesses—rain, chill, and the labor of hauling the wood chips and moving rocks. From indoors, I realize, all those unpleasantries are just thoughts. They are only thoughts. They come. They go.

Once I've bundled up in my garden coat, and put on boots and garden gloves, I walk outdoors into bird-singing spring.

DAPHNE BLOOMS

Daphne is blooming in my garden now; its tiny sweet blossoms make it the earliest flowering shrub. In the Pacific Northwest, where I once lived, the long, long spring commences when daphne begins blooming at the end of January. Here in the Northeast, it does not flower till mid-April.

We all bloom at different times—in beauty and in relationship. So, too, our meditation practice blooms differently for each person. I still have not had some of the most elementary insights.

Impermanence is one of the very first insights—noticing constant change. Although I know impermanence intellectually, I don't know it in a bone-shaking sort of way. *OMG, there's **nothing** to hang on to.*

Daphne will teach me in her own gentle way. She blooms, and soon, very soon, those lovely white blossoms begin to spot and turn brown. Sort of like my own aging skin. Then the flowers fall to earth.

EYE-CATCHING GOLD

The shrub *Physocarpus* (a.k.a. Ninebark) is leafing out. I have two varieties. Dart's Gold looks like forsythia from a distance, but this shrub's bright yellow-green leaves color the garden for weeks longer than forsythia, whose flowers are already dropping to the ground.

My other variety is "Summer Wine" whose red-purple leaves create a nice accent on an otherwise green background.

I particularly like the eye-catching yellow-green leaves of Dart's Gold, which draw my attention, no matter where I am in the garden. The rest of the garden is spring-beautiful and delightful to walk around in, yet Physocarpus overwhelms my visual field and completely stops my wandering eyes.

As we approach concentration in our meditation, our attention is captured by something pleasant and delightful in the body-mind. When joy arises, delight in it, fill yourself with it. Joy comes before concentration.

Awaken joy and awaken yourself.

"SO GOOD TO SEE YOU. CAN YOU REMIND ME WHAT YOUR NAME IS?"

In late April, my old friends, my perennials, poke out their heads to say, "Hello again." I am *so* happy to see them, one by one. But, just like acquaintances I haven't seen for several months, I can't remember their names.

I smile and open my arms wide. "So good to see you again, uh-uh-uh.

Can you remind me what your name is?"

Not knowing someone's name is an unpleasant sensation. I love knowing. I love to *know* things, and I especially love to know names. Between now and when a flower's name comes to me, I focus on how the bloom looks and recall that just after it rains, her mantle-leaf catches jewel-like raindrops. She's a mistress of alchemy, this one, as she turns water into chem-istry.

Minutes or hours later, the name comes to me, and that memory/thought is a pleasant feeling, all by itself. Oh yes! *Alchemilla* (al-Camilla?), Lady's Mantle. Her name evokes a pleasant feeling—and now, finally, I can welcome her into the garden by name.

CONTENT WITH HELLEBORE

Many gardeners love *Hellebore orientalis* for its early, wild-rose-like flower and evergreen foliage. *Hellebore orientalis* is also called Lenten Rose, but that must be someone else's Lent, because it doesn't bloom here until weeks after Lent.

My favorite hellebore is *niger,* also known as Christmas Rose. *Hellebore niger* blooms earlier than *orientalis,* but is hard to find at the nursery, so I have to be content with the single clump that sprouts in my bland-looking flowerbed, appearing like a white bouquet of five-petaled dogwood.

Contentment is a form of wishlessness, not longing for things to be different. I say I have to be content with my single clump, but underneath, I *do* long for more, more, more *Hellebore niger.* That is not contentment.

Contentment sees *Hellebore niger* and loves it as it is, whether or not there is ever any more, more, more.

THE RABBIT TRAILS OF INTENTIONS

I hopped out of bed with the intention of planting four dozen onions. I planted a six-pack of chard instead.

But before doing that, I went down the rabbit trail of cleaning up the little bed I am transplanting the chard into. This meant I had to dig up the flowers that had sown themselves there—feverfew, lamium, and woodland poppies. In order to pot up those flowers, so I can give them away, I needed to screen my young compost. Forty-five minutes later, the chard was planted and the onions were still patiently sitting there, looking at me.

This sounds rather like our meditation practice some days. Perhaps we get out of bed late and just want to hit the computer to check the weather or send an email. Forty-five minutes and many rabbit trails later, we're not even dressed for work, and our time for meditation has evaporated.

Or our life. We intend a spiritual practice, but life! So much to do. Loved ones to care for and worry about. The mortgage to pay. Forty-five years later, where are we?

We're still in the present moment. And Life is patiently looking at us, smiling.

PRACTICING GARDENING

When we say "practice the piano," we don't expect the results to be perfect. Part of developing a skill is making a lot of "wrong moves." In this way, we train our bodies and minds to move skillfully.

We have a meditation practice too, training our minds to move in skillful ways, beginning with mindfulness and loving-kindness.

Gardening is also a practice. No one is perfect at it, not even the so-called experts. We practice by planting seeds or seedlings, annuals or perennials. As much as we might like to "do it right," we have to make a lot of "mistakes," a lot of "wrong moves." That's the reason I'm digging up that blue hydrangea I planted four years ago, and moving it to a sunnier location.

photo credit: kazoka30 / iStock

COLD WIND

A cold front with strong winds blew in one late April, tearing old leaves from the beech trees. The wind raked leaves across the lawn and into the woods, then changed its mind, switched directions, and blew them across the lawn to the other side. The air was thick with flying dead leaves.

Sometimes our cold heart rakes old, dead wrongs back and forth across our mind. The winds of blame and pain blow strong, and it seems we are at the mercy of our changeable mind.

Stop. Don't blame the trigger. Let go. Substitute the opposite. Loving-kindness warms the heart and cools the mind.

Stopping the mind from the rampage of the cold front is a hard assignment. We may want to present an air of aloofness to the world with an unfeeling "Whatever."

Dare to feel that unpleasant, oh-so-uncomfortable emotion. Find the sensation in the body. Name the emotion if you can, but if you can't, don't worry.

Sink into the ouchy sensation. Press into it with mindfulness like an acupressure point. Watch the mind/pain let go of its own accord. Apply the balm of loving-kindness.

CHASING THE PLEASANT

My plants have been like pets this week. Outdoors. Indoors. Outdoors. Indoors. Now that the freezing weather has ended, they can go outdoors—and stay there.

People around here are returning from a week of spring vacation, but for my plants, summer vacation is beginning.

Our own constant motion is an attempt to find a pleasant place to abide in. But pleasantness is fleeting. Our bodies keep chasing warmth—sometimes flying thousands of miles to find it. Or we chase coolness. We chase comfort. When we sit still, our body in meditation, our mind continues to chase pleasantness by daydreaming or dozing.

Come home to your body. Rest right here in its changing sensations. Come home to the mind and its kaleidoscope of changing thoughts.

Allow pleasantness to come and go, the way it always does.

NATURALIZING MINDFULNESS

I grew up in the rich woods of the Midwest. On May Day, my sister and I picked bouquets of Dutchman's breeches, jack-in-the-pulpit, wild phlox, and spring beauties.

Years ago, when I moved to my home in the dry pine woods of Vermont, I tried repeatedly to grow the wildflowers of my childhood. No luck.

Eventually one of my shaded nursery beds, under an old apple tree, turned out to be the perfect place for Dutchman's breeches—which look like little white pantaloons with pale yellow pockets turned inside out, a week's worth of laundry hanging upside-down on a clothesline stem. I stopped planting other wildflowers in that bed and gave Dutchman's breeches free rein.

The Dutchman's breeches have jumped into another flowerbed, about a hundred feet away from where I am carefully colonizing them. This process of naturalizing a wildflower makes me very happy.

So, too, we try to naturalize mindfulness in our lives. It isn't easy. It's challenge enough to be mindful when we're practicing sitting meditation. How can we possibly practice mindfulness at work or in the car or on the phone or on the computer?

We keep meditating, practicing mindfulness, and then, one day, it pops up while we are taking a walk. There it is. Mindfulness in our daily life, naturalizing itself.

I am delighted that the Dutchman's breeches have naturalized into the woodland. Mindfulness is another name for happiness; may it naturalize itself in our daily lives.

MEDITATING WITH A SQUIRREL

The meditation center where I teach is sponsoring a May Meditation Challenge and sending out daily inspirational messages. For those who have a sporadic practice, the goal is to sit every day. If you have an established practice, you're encouraged to sit twice a day. I've taken on the challenge of sitting outdoors every day.

I do love sitting on my deck and listening to the chorus of birds singing all around me—robins whinnying and rose-breasted grosbeaks singing their arias to the percussion of woodpeckers. This morning, a gray squirrel sat two feet away from me. Her fluffy gray tail curled over her smooth gray-brown coat as if to keep her warm. I watched her breathing, and, with her big, round, unblinking brown eyes, she watched me breathing.

I can hardly wait to go meditate on my deck again.

photo credit: Jill Y Nightingale / iStock

THE MONTH OF MAY

Twenty years ago today, I graduated from Antioch University New England with a Master's degree in Counseling. As a reward to myself, I dedicated the month to gardening. Then I started my job hunt in June.

Whenever I can, I love dedicating May as my major gardening month. What a great excuse to be outdoors, watching flowers come and go, my finger on the pulse of life.

I retreat from the house into the garden. I retreat from the virtual world of the computer to the real world of nature.

Like any meditation retreat, time in the garden really slows down my world and calms my mind.

Treat yourself to a retreat from the world of stress and busy-ness. Take a mindful moment retreat right now.

MY HERB GARDEN CHANGES—AND VANISHES

A local garden club tours my spring garden in early May. Does my garden look good? Of course. It's spring! I have lots of spring-blooming flowers—*Leucojum* (summer snowflake), *Lunaria* (money plant), and *Phlox divercata* (woodland phlox) accent the spaces between the narcissus and jonquils.

Do I feel ready for the garden tour? Of course not. My herb garden is half torn apart due to excavation, which will start tomorrow.

Everything I cherish will change and vanish. My dear herb garden is changing and vanishing. Next month, two trenches will be dug through it to connect utilities from the house to a little guest room attached to the garage we are building. Tomorrow, four feet of dirt will be piled on top of the back half of the herb garden. It will be a mess out there. Now, it's just a pre-mess.

Everything I cherish will change and vanish, including myself. These "little" changes are just preparing me for the big event.

WELL-COMPOSTED MANURE

On Saturday, I drove to a nearby farm and picked up a truckload of manure. I intended to top off my compost piles, but the manure was already so well composted that I decided to shovel it directly onto my vegetable garden and the surrounding strip beds.

I find the occasional un-decomposed woody stem. I've been to Farmer Charlie's manure piles often enough to recognize the remains of a three-foot- tall lamb's quarters or other weed. Yes, there are probably a zillion weed seeds in this gorgeously composted manure.

We go shopping. We find something beautiful. We buy it and bring it home. We don't recognize the stress that is inherent in this new thing, which turns into clutter or becomes something we don't even see. New clothes! How wonderful! Until our drawers are overflowing, and our closets are stuffed. In the morning, we lie in bed for an extra 15 or 30 minutes just trying to figure out what to wear. New clothes are stress in sheep's clothing.

But for now, the vegetable garden is beautiful with its cover of rich, dark, well-composted manure.

GARDENING UNTIL DARK

Gardening in the morning,
Gardening in the evening,
Gardening at suppertime.

I gardened until dark last evening. What a joy to be outdoors until 8:15! So much better than sitting in the house or at the computer.

Some mornings I'm out in the garden at 5:00 A.M., immersed in the warbling of birds, the cool damp, and the light in the eastern sky. Chickadees talk to me, saying "Sweet. Sweet. Sweet."

This is what happiness feels like. En-joy-ment. Grateful to be in the garden. A little fountain of love running over in my heart. Sweet.

photo credit: Jurgute / iStock

RELAX INTO SPRING

If there is such a thing as full spring, May is it. Cool and breezy, with the sun warm enough to help you shed that jacket or other outer layer. Azaleas and rhododendrons are in bloom. My neighbor's white azalea looks like a snowbank. Birds are singing and building their nests in the branches.

Meditation also helps us shed our outer layer—that first layer of armor—defensiveness, anxiety, worry, bother, frustration, or irritation. Whatever your particular brand of armor against the world, the first meditation instruction is:

Relax.

Relax the body and allow the mind to remain alert. The body doesn't need to be on alert. The body doesn't need to be vigilant. The body doesn't have to be poised to spring into action.

The first loving-kindness phrase is "May I feel safe." Feel safe now.

In your body. In this room. In your home. In your garden. In your neighborhood.

Relax into spring. Relax into the kind friendliness that is all around you.

SUMMER VACATION

Summer vacation begins early for my houseplants, as it does for students in rural counties whose schools let out early so the kids can work on the farm. I grew up next to a cornfield and a soybean field. My school year ended in mid-May. A generation earlier, my Depression-era farmboy father graduated from high school on April 30, 1936.

My houseplants have been cooped up indoors since September and are looking a bit peaked despite frequent trips to the water fountain and lunches of fish emulsion.

Outdoors, houseplants love being exposed to the elements—rain and wind strengthen their leaves and roots, which burrow ever more deeply into the earthy soil of their flowerpots. Although sheltered from direct sun, the houseplants catch the bouncing rays.

Earth, air, water, warmth. We ourselves are made of the same stuff as geraniums and jade plants.

HONESTY

Now that the daffodils are almost finished blooming, tulips usually take up the slack. But I gave up planting tulips years ago, because I was tired of waging war on bulb-eating chipmunks. I so much more enjoy watching chippies scamper around the flowerbeds than growling at them for their culinary predilections.

Purple-pink money plant (*Lunaria*) and white summer snowflake (*Leucojum*) are blooming all over my garden now. They have been flowering for three weeks and will continue for another three. I do like flowers that last a long time.

Money plant is also called *honesty*. One aspect of honesty consists of speaking truthfully and helpfully. What we are about to say may well be true, but, we need to ask ourselves: is it helpful?

Can we cultivate the skill of "straightforward and gentle" speech? Sometimes we refrain from speaking the truth in order not to hurt another person's feelings. Here we're walking a fine line, so I frequently reflect on how "straight-forward and gentle" applies to my current situation. I need not sacrifice honesty for gentleness; nor do I need to sacrifice gentleness for truth.

Honesty "holds" the bloom in my garden during this mid-spring season. I work on holding the bloom of honesty in all my relationships.

PEONY SUPPORTS

I am placing tomato cages (the smallest ones) around my peonies. Tomato cages may not be especially attractive, but they cost one-tenth the price of those fancy green metal plant supports. Besides, I have dozens of tomato cages, dozens of peonies, and only a couple of plant supports.

The tomato cages look rather out of place now while the peonies are growing, but within two weeks, the cages will be invisible. More importantly, they will prevent heavy-blossomed peonies from drooping in the wind or rain.

When you are new to meditation, you also need supports. Guided meditations—on a CD or downloaded to your iPod, tablet, or smartphone—are good for keeping you on track and on the cushion. You might go to Dharma Seed (great name!) (www.dharmaseed.org) to find a teacher or subject that interests you.

Meditating with friends once a week is also a wonderful support. Do you have a certain friend or a few friends with whom you could share a moment of silence—when you see each other, on the phone, or before eating a meal? "Let's just share a moment of silence together, because I really want to *be here* with you."

Reading inspirational books is another support, as are taking a class or attending a talk or a public sitting, if they are offered in your town.

Yes, at first these supports may feel as clunky as tomato cages, but in just a couple of weeks, they'll be your "spiritual friends," supporting you on the path to a more peaceful life.

MULCH HAY

I picked up a truckload of mulch hay yesterday to use on the vegetable garden. It took nerve, but, about ten years ago, I converted to the Ruth Stout method after watching the video "Ruth Stout's Garden." In the 1976 video, ninety-two-year-old Ruth hobbles along on her cane, but she still gardens. She can't bend over to pull a weed, so she plops a big handful of straw or hay on every weed she sees. She smothers the weed and improves the soil at the same time.

We can do the same thing with weedy thoughts. We can "kill them with kindness." By practicing loving-kindness or patience, we lay to rest a moment of weedy irritation.

Eight bales of rotting hay will smother a lot of weeds in the vegetable garden.

SUDDENLY HOT

Suddenly, it's hot by midday. I dash out to the garden in the early daylight to work while it's cool. By 11:00, I change from sweatpants into long cotton pants. Then, an hour later, I change into shorts.

My neighbor, Whit, doesn't like to change clothes during the day, so I sometimes see him in shorts when it's 43 degrees. I'm covered up in a fleece jacket, hat, and gloves while he's in short sleeves. Some of us like change; some of us don't.

Right now, I'm waiting for my broccoli seeds to change into seedlings. Meanwhile, the daffodils are wilting and changing into deadheads.

Change is happening every moment, whether we like it or not.

CURTAILING THE IMPULSE TO BUY, BUY, BUY

This spring, with so much construction happening here and so much deconstruction of the herb garden, I'm renouncing buying plants. Well, let's say I'm renouncing going overboard. So far, I have bought pansies, onion plants, grape and Sun Gold cherry tomatoes, and one variegated impatiens.

I bring my small haul home and don't stop at the garden center again until I've planted what I have. This step-by-step method really slows down my purchasing. The fringe benefit is that it's good for my pocketbook.

Curtailing my impulse to buy, buy, buy feels like going against the grain. Desire wants to spring into spring with all its hope and promise. Desire doesn't always have our best interests at heart. My heart rests easier with less planting to do. My heart is happier with less.

photo credit: Buba1955 / iStock

BUMPING INTO THE GLASS CEILING

Before my sweetie put the screen doors on, I was traipsing in and out of the solarium, taking the house-plants outdoors for their summer vacation. The next time I was in the solarium, I heard *Bzzzz, bzzzz.* A big old bumblebee was searching for a way out. He kept hitting up against the glass ceiling. The outdoors *looked* so close.

We too hit up against the glass of our own stress, not even recognizing stress as stress. In my twenties and thirties, I thought I could practice "sexual freedom," as I then called it. Pain and suffering inevitably followed. Still, I bumbled on, hitting up against the glass of stress. Why couldn't I just get through it? Other people seemed to have a lot of fun. It took years to understand my experience. It took years to begin to practice refraining from sexual misconduct.

We worry about loved ones, and call that worry "love." Worry is stress; love is stress-free.

Eventually, I captured the bumblebee under a glass and whisked him outdoors.

Let's allow our minds the freedom of true love—wide open and spacious.

GERMANDER. GONE.

I'm ripping germander out of my patio garden. It's a good little edging, adaptable to poor and dry soils. I originally liked it because it is an evergreen herb used in European knot gardens. But the fact is, germander is toxic as an herb, and I don't have a knot garden, nor a British garden.

Germander offers a brief bloom of tiny pink flowers—and its tiny green scalloped leaves just do not provide enough sense pleasure.

Sense pleasures are quite temporary, lasting only a few seconds, I realize. Yet, we spend much of our lives chasing such pleasures—one more pretty thing, a song we can rock to, being near friends whom we text—and then they're gone. Such fleeting pleasures provide only surface happiness. Deep happiness also exists, and we can shift our course to aim more precisely at the happiness that is available to us even if outer circumstances are poor and dry. This deep happiness is an inner happiness.

Today, my deep happiness comes from the practice of generosity. I'm giving my germander away to someone who really wants it.

70% HUMIDITY

Rain. Fog. Mist. Drizzle. Overcast.

Gray skies. Rain splattering in mud puddles. Fog obscuring my view. When the rain stops, I walk outdoors and feel soggy.

The humidity today is about 70%. Since the body is 70% water, perhaps we could say that the "humidity" of the body is 70%.

What if we could "see" the mist of the body? Mist has no boundaries, but permeates everything, everywhere.

What if we viewed our bodies not as distinct entities, but as part of the environment surrounding us? Would that cause us to see our bodies, see the planet differently?

What if we could see that there is no such thing as "my" water? What if we noticed that "my" water is the same as all the other water around us? What if we saw "my" water flowing into the world around us and water from the world around us flowing into us?

Rain. Fog. Mist. Drizzle. Water, water everywhere, and not a drop to call "mine."

GRACEFUL VIBURNUM

Double-file viburnum is in bloom. This architectural shrub grows up to eight feet tall. Its "arms" reach out horizontally another eight feet, with clusters of white wrist corsages covering the arms, all the way to the "shoulder." The dancer-like grace of this shrub thrills every visitor.

I planted this white-blooming shrub between a magenta rhododendron and a raspberry-colored rhododendron. Place white between any two "hard" colors, and you'll see that the latter suddenly get along with each other. We could say white is a cure-all.

So, too, mindfulness is a cure-all we can bring to any situation. Take any difficult feeling and name it, mindfully. Repeatedly label it as you focus your attention on the physical sensations in the body. Feel the uncomfortable, unpleasant sensations—mindfully. The mind will want to escape into a big, long story. Try, instead, to gently attend to the pain in the mind and body.

Sometimes, bringing mindful attention to bodily sensations can help us work with difficult feelings and thoughts. Then we become aware of the galloping mind itself, as we repeatedly re-tether the mind to the body.

Mindfulness "cures" us (one moment at a time) of the next desire or the next hard judgment we were about lay on someone. Mindfulness adds grace to our words and to our actions.

COMMUNITY GARDEN COMPARISON

Last week someone mowed along the edge of the community garden, revealing that my plot was the only one with tall grass, dock, and mustard growing up through the fence. My comparing mind couldn't help but notice that my helter-skelter plot was not conforming to the nicely groomed look of the other eleven plots.

So yesterday I finally brought my garden fork there. As I uprooted each clump of weeds, I'd sneak a look at the neighbors' plots, where tiny lettuces grew in neat rows. Thanks to a heavy dose of manure last year, my own plot was teeming, not only with grass, dock, and mustard, but with clover and lambs' quarters, as well.

The mind loves to compare. In fact, that's really all it does. *Am I better than…* or *Am I worse than…?* The ego loves these mind games, which give rise to various forms of pride and ill will (generally toward oneself). What if things simply are as they are, without judgment, without comparison?

Tranquility, calm, and peace do not thrive in a weedy mind that is busy comparing itself to others. Can you bring non-judgmental awareness to the present moment?

Begin by pausing to name the weeds in your mind: impatience, irritation, daydreaming, planning, worrying, anxiety, or what have you. Sometimes, that's all we have to do—just name those weedy thoughts. This helps us to begin uprooting it.

TRANSPLANTING STRESS

A friend who works on an organic farm brought home two trays of lettuce six-packs to give away. The seedlings are not only ready to be transplanted, they are ready to be eaten.

This makes gardening so easy: transplant the lettuce into your garden and begin harvesting immediately. Wouldn't we like to transplant stress reduction or a spiritual practice into our already too-busy lives? Wouldn't we like to harvest the fruits (or vegetables!) of a spiritual practice right *now*?

"If I just accomplish this one more thing, I'll have less stress," we think. Question this belief.

Transplanting a spiritual practice often requires that we begin by renouncing something. We can't take care of a burgeoning garden of things-we-want-to-do without collapsing under the weight. Instead of desperately attempting to maintain a way-too-big garden of busyness, we can tend just as much as our tender hearts can open to.

photo credit: AlexRaths / iStock

GARDENER'S NOSE

I went to the dermatologist last week to have her freeze a couple of spots on my face—a scaly spot and a red bump, both of which were precancerous. I asked her to look at my nose, which feels a bit rough. "Oh, you've got gardener's nose," she said.

Often our skin is not beautiful. It's bumpy, scaly, rough in patches, and, like mine, a bit wrinkly. Look, really look at your skin with a magnifying glass.

During a recent meditation retreat, the monk/teacher led us through an abbreviated body meditation. First, he asked us to visualize our skin. "Not beautiful," he pronounced. Then our flesh. All I could imagine was the meat department at the grocery store. "Not beautiful," he repeated. Then our bones. "Not beautiful," he said.

Our skin is a cling wrap that covers the body. It peels, it scales off, it sweats, it wrinkles. Our skin is the bag that holds the innards of our body together. Your bag looks like that; my bag looks like this.

I'm taking my bag and my gardener's nose out to the garden to breathe in the spring air and smell the flowers while I can.

THE ILLUSION OF CONTROL

In May, while the growing season is still young, our hearts open wide to our gardens. We train them toward what we imagine will be their perfect beauty and yield.

The willfulness of weeds and the proliferation of the young plants is only beginning. We think we can keep up with them.

Alas! The youthful vigor of our gardens exceeds our own energy. Try as we may, with our busy workaday and family lives, we cannot keep up. We leave our latchkey gardens to their own devices. By July, we'll be clucking our tongues over their unruly behavior. "What can we do?" we'll say to our friends.

Right now, in May, we are in love, we believe in our hopes and dreams for the future, and that is sufficient.

THRIVING IN THE RIGHT-FOR-US LOCATION

Three years ago, I transplanted saruma to a different location, under the eaves on the north side of the house. There, in total shade, it has multiplied, generating a couple of dozen babies.

Meanwhile, I seem to have lost the "grandmother plant" in the original location.

In order to bloom, we have to be in the right-for-us location. Many, many other plants would languish under the eaves on the north side, but saruma thrives. I thrive in a situation with just a few social contacts. My meditation practice thrives when I have less "to-do" in my life.

Where do you thrive? Where and when does your meditation practice thrive?

photo credit: John Richmond / Alamy Stock Photo

GENEROSITY CANCELS GREED

The library has a Book & Plant Sale on Memorial Day weekend. What a great opportunity to donate a pile of books I am not going to read again. It's also an excellent opportunity to stroll through the garden, trowel in hand, digging up plants that are too crowded or that have volunteered in the "wrong" places. In the vegetable garden, I had four square feet of dill that reseeded itself. That's a *lot* of dill. I potted it up in two flats of six-packs.

Generosity, giving things away, cancels out greed. I used to collect books. I thought more books was good. Then I took a hard look at my wall of books. It really wasn't very pretty. Is that what I thought my brain looked like?

I used to collect plants, adding new plants and watching older ones spread naturally; but, after thirty years, my flowerbeds are full to overflowing. In order to put something in, I now realize, I have to take something—or a few somethings—out.

Let's take several things out of the flower and vegetable gardens and give them away. Let them multiply in someone else's garden, and the joy of giving will multiply in our heart.

TENDER PERENNIALS (SO-CALLED)

I ran into my friend Barbara at the garden center. She didn't see me at first, because she was studying the lavenders with a wrinkled brow.

"Barbara!" I said.

Her face lit up and relaxed as she re-cognized me. At least something here was familiar. "You can help me," she said confidently. "Which lavender should I buy?"

Hmmm. I started my lavender from seed 33 years ago, and the name on the little brown seed packet is lost in the mists of time. Now it was my turn to study the white plastic markers.

Provence lavender sounded wonderful, but wait a minute. The small print said, "Tender Perennial." Greek lavender bore the same description—Tender Perennial.

Well, the Provence and Greek lavenders might be perennial three climate zones and 800 miles south of here. "Tender Perennial" is simply code that means "annual." Here in Vermont, the only way these varieties of lavender—or rosemary, for that matter—are perennial is if you dig them up and bring them into the house in September.

This sort of stretching of truth is actually a form of lying. Its goal is to mislead the customer. "Tender Perennial" does not qualify as skillful speech. "Tender Perennial" simply means that you, the consumer, have to perennially treat this plant as tenderly as a baby. Since I have dozens of plant "children" (okay, thousands), this baby will most likely be lost to frost in the fall.

Barbara and I settled on *Lavandula angustifolia* "Hidcote" or "Munstead" as being most hardy, but the lavender mood had passed, and she walked away without buying anything.

DONE!

I reached the bottom of one compost pile. Oh, how wonderful to finally see that black plastic "floor." I put the "gate" (the fourth pallet) back on that bin and immediately began filling it up again. The next day, my gardening friend Melissa and I hauled two garden-cartloads of lamium to that bin, so it's about one-third full already.

Now I'm screening my way through the middle bin, using the compost to pot up plants I've thinned out of my flowerbeds.

I feel a certain sense of accomplishment when I finish a project—or finish a compost bin. *There. That's done.* But, of course, it isn't done. It's gone. That compost pile is gone. The other thing that's gone is my desire to finish, to accomplish that particular thing. Desire has evaporated, and it feels *so* good to be desireless for a moment.

So what do I do? Start all over again. New compost pile. New desire. New wanting-to-finish. New stress, mild though it may be.

Simply recognize stress, in all its disguises. Recognize the truth of life.

SPRINKLING LIFE WITH MINDFULNESS

I came home from the Garden Club plant sale with a sprinkler. Another sprinkler. I am weary of buying plastic sprinklers that stop oscillating for one reason or another. Fortunately, this sprinkler was free.

I like to have a sprinkler near every outdoor faucet for ease of access. Likewise, when the hot weather of life stresses us, it's helpful to have a mindfulness practice to cool our churning thoughts and emotions.

When we are stressed by traffic, co-workers, anxiety about the future, or worry about the past, can we slowly and attentively bring our mind to the present moment? One way to do this is to focus on the breath, on the in and out, the inhalations and exhalations of the body.

We might also practice some loving-kindness. Here is a loving-kindness verse you might whisper to yourself in your mind: *May I feel safe. May I feel happy. May I feel peaceful.*

Wherever you are—at the kitchen sink, in the car, or in the garden—simply become aware of the body breathing or the body standing or sitting or bending over.

Sprinkle your life with mindfulness.

WEEDING THE CRACKS

I'm using my weeder—a long, pointy metal dowel with a handle—to weed between the cracks of my fieldstone walkways.

I like to see creeping thyme or Irish moss or cute little mazus growing in the cracks. But the flowers (or weeds) that volunteer there are more likely to be tall phlox or prolific spiderwort. Bleeding heart likes to grow in the cracks of my stone steps.

The weeder is a great tool for getting down into those spots where a trowel won't go. Wiggle, wiggle, wiggle. The soil loosens, and the plant pops out *with* its roots attached. Whew!

What are the weeds that grow in the cracks of our lives? I'm sure you know these "familiars"— complaining, judging, desiring, anticipating, hoping, dreaming.

First, let's use the tool of mindfulness to identify that weed (a plant growing in the wrong place, or a stressful thought). Sometimes, just noticing—"Irritation. Irritation." or "Hi, Judge"—is sufficient for the thought to dissipate.

But there are some thoughts that come back and back and back. Here's where we need the "weeder" to pry into that thought. How does that thought feel in the body? Where in the body do you feel that thought? Focus, really focus on the sensations of that thought/feeling. What do you notice?

Sink into that sensation/feeling. Allow your attention to be completely consumed by it. What happens?

One by one, we pry stressful thoughts out of our lives. One step at a time, we become happier.

I'D RATHER BE....

Company's coming on Sunday, so I'm prissing up the flowerbeds when I'd rather be out in the vegetable garden trying to get it under control. (As if that were possible.)

This double-mindedness afflicts our every waking moment, and is summed up by those bumper stickers that say, "I'd rather be...."

Sometimes we don't get around to meditating, because we'd rather stay in bed (in the morning) or watch TV (in the evening). We think we're reducing our stress by doing something pleasant, but the real stress reduction comes from calm and tranquil mindfulness, not from mindless vegging out.

When in the flowerbed, just attend to the flowers. When in the veggie garden, just take care of the vegetables.

photo credit: shutterstock

ANTI-INFLAMMATORY KALE & MINDFULNESS

Red Russian kale has reseeded itself not only in the vegetable garden, but also in other nearby beds. I have hundreds of kale plants, and wish I could send you some.

As it is, I'm patiently potting them into six-packs to take to the Perennial Swappers meeting. I know from experience that a couple dozen Swappers will only take so much kale, so I'll have to compost most of the seedlings.

I am rich in kale. Kale is so rich in vitamins and minerals that it's called a superfood. Ounce for ounce, it contains:

1. More iron than beef.
2. More calcium than milk.
3. Ten times more Vitamin C than spinach.
4. Incredible anti-inflammatory properties. (Inflammation is a major cause of heart disease.)

So, too, mindfulness is a superfood for the heart and mind, because it has the ability to cut down and then replace inflammatory thoughts. The days I don't meditate are the days when I become irritated with something or someone.

Eat more kale; it's good for the heart. Practice more mindfulness; it's good for the heart and mind.

THE HOSPICE MEMORIAL GARDEN

Our local hospice has a memorial garden, and every year offers a planting ceremony for the community. Nearby garden centers each donate a flat or two of annuals, so the recently bereaved can plant a petunia, a marigold, or some other flower in memory of a loved one. Some people bring their own perennials to plant. My neighbor, for instance, is taking daisies from my garden to plant in memory of her Aunt Daisy.

There's something primal about planting a flower in the earth to remember the dear departed, whose bodies have either been planted in cemeteries or had their cremains sprinkled over earth or water.

At the hospice garden, you can write the name of your loved one on a flat rock as big as the palm of your hand, and place this "tombstone" next to whatever you have just planted. All the while, a dulcimer plays softly.

In this season, when plants are practically leaping out of the ground, we take time to remember where we came from ourselves. We also may remember those we've planted in the earth this past year.

Now, in this season of birth and blooming, we recall those who have already returned to the great recycling machine of Earth.

LITTLE BY LITTLE

Every May, Melissa asks me over to her house for lunch. But first, we stroll through her gardens, and I give her ideas for what to plant where or what to move where. Her backyard is quite shady, and when I first visited, she was frustrated by the underperformance of the full-sun plants she loves.

After that, she focused on her backdoor garden, and she soon had a lovely shade garden with hosta, hellebore, and bloodroot. This year, her front door garden is stunning, with a sweet woodruff ground cover.

On this most recent visit, I drove into her driveway, parked beside her car, and looked across the yard to a colorful, partially sunny wet spot. Delightful.

Poco a poco, little by little, Melissa becomes happier with her various flowerbeds.

Over time, we can focus on different themes in our meditation: the breathing, hearing, sensations of the body, and loving-kindness. Day by day and year by year, our inner meditation garden grows richer and deeper.

And our meditation becomes a pleasure.

BLACK LOCUST TREES

Black locust trees are in bloom, and the whole town smells heavenly. The dangling panicles of creamy white flowers, which look like wisteria, emit a sweet fragrance that honeybees love.

We went to our favorite outdoor chicken & ribs grill on a bluff overlooking a river, and sat at a picnic table under a black locust. Oh, my!

Though we seldom have the opportunity to be so mindful of smells, let's notice the details of smelling. Where in the nose do you "feel" a smell? How long does it take for the nose to acclimate to the fragrance?

Who knew that heaven was as close as walking outdoors?

photo credit: martypatch / iStock

LABELING

Since I can't bear to throw plants away, I pot up my extras to give away. Then I use popsicle sticks to label them. "Yellow daylily" or "Russian sage."

In meditation, it's helpful to label your distracting thoughts. You have several ways to do this:

You can simply identify a thought as involving the "past" or the "future."

Or you can note the nature of a thought. Does it consist of "planning"? "Worrying"? "Daydreaming"?

Another approach would be to note or label what in particular hinders your meditation. Is it:

- sense desire
- ill-will
- lethargy & sleepiness
- restlessness & worry
- doubt

Just as labeling plants helps the recipient to know what plants she is receiving, labeling your thoughts increases your mindfulness.

SIMPLIFY YOUR FLOWERBED

My inclination with flowerbeds is to cultivate small clusters of flowers near the house, which become larger the farther away you go. By the house, I allow a clump of flowers to grow no more than a foot in diameter; farther away, I let colonies grow two to three feet in diameter.

In practice this means ongoing division and completely removing "spreaders" (such as beebalm or phlox) from the neat little beds. The success of this sort of limitation all depends on your tolerance for dividing. Some gardeners can't bear to divide their flowers at all.

Flowers can overwhelm our little gardens, just as stuff can overwhelm our homes and multi-tasking can overwhelm our lives.

Simplify your garden, your house or apartment, and your to-do list. Create some breathing space for your plants and yourself. What one thing can you let go of today?

Maybe it's the spreaders in your garden.

WANTING SOMETHING DIFFERENT

Yesterday I had one hour to spend in my community garden plot. My plan was to turn over the last third of the garden, plant Brussels sprout and red cabbage seedlings, then plant turnip and rutabaga seeds. And that's as far as I got. The other four things on my to-do list would have taken another hour.

Since I don't usually garden by the clock, I was surprised that my body couldn't accomplish all that the mind had planned for it. I was also surprised by how time-less the garden is.

Sure, when I'm home, I often squeeze in a few gardening chores before driving off to an appointment, but I know I'll be back that day or the next. My community garden plot is a ten-minute drive from home, and I know I won't return to it for a few days. Planting the squash and the Sun Gold cherry tomatoes will have to wait.

"Waiting" is when stress arises. I want something (planting) that cannot be had right now. Impatience, frustration, and anxiety arise—more stress.

I enjoyed a lovely, time-less hour in the garden, chatting with another gardener working in her plot. That calm was then overwhelmed by the desire for things to be different from how they were.

Wisdom accepts things just as they are: plot turned over, seedlings transplanted, seeds planted. Ahh! A beautiful breezy day interlude in the sunny garden.

RED-BELLIED WOODPECKER

A red-bellied woodpecker now lives nearby. Till recently, I'd never seen this sleek orange-headed bird in our neighborhood. At first, I thought it was a flicker (they're on adjoining pages of my bird book), but then I looked more carefully at the distinguishing marks. Surprise! It's a red-bellied woodpecker, which actually has just a small tinge of pale red on its belly.

Our minds can fool us too. Then we look more closely at a particular idea and discover that things are not what we thought they were.

Desire feels good. But look closely at those desiring thoughts—desires for your children or grandchildren, desire for a vacation. We recall the pleasantness and bring it to mind time and again. Then we realize: desire is a not as pleasant as we thought it was.

Take a closer look. Work on identifying those thoughts. Are they useful? Or useless?

Things are not as they seem. Let's aim to see life as it really is.

photo credit: abriggs21 / iStock

REPLANT AGAIN

My summer squash seeds still have not sprouted. Well, they were packaged eight years ago, so I had expected a low germination rate. But I'd hoped it wouldn't be zero percent. Sigh. It's time to replant.

I just finished teaching an eight-week class called "Begin Again." The students all had previous meditation experience, but meditation had fallen away from their lives. So, they began again, as we all do, every time we sit down on the cushion.

It's time to replant our intention to meditate. What do you aspire to?

In the garden, I aspire to a crop of summer squash (my favorite!). In meditation, I aspire to daily sitting. I am inspired by the Dalai Lama, who arises at 3 A.M. and meditates for three hours before turning on the BBC World News. What a great way to start the day.

I've already started my day with a long sit and by writing this journal entry. Now it's time to walk out into this summer day and plant summer squash.

THIRST-QUENCHING ICED MINT TEA

Every evening, after dinner, while my sweetie is doing the dishes, I walk out the back door to the mint patch. Last year's construction (and two trenches through the former herb garden) gave the mint free rein, so the mint bed is now about eight feet long and six feet wide. W-a-y too big.

I pull up five or six stems of mint by the roots, clip off the roots, and bring the mint indoors to make iced mint tea for tomorrow. This year I've been adding hibiscus flowers and a touch of maple syrup for a truly thirst-quenching drink on hot afternoons.

When we pull up the roots of stress (greed, aversion, and delusion), our craving, our thirst, will be quenched.

We could look at our inner mint patch and sigh in despair. Or we could put ourselves on a daily diet of meditation and mindfulness and mint tea. Little by little, the inner heat cools to a refreshing joy.

TOO HOT TO TRANSPLANT

Transplanting season is over. As we enter the hottest 90 days of the year (June 9 to September 9), the weather becomes too hot and dry to safely transplant.

Oh, you can still transplant if you really want to. You just have to watch that transplant as if it's a baby—water it daily, or maybe twice a day, perhaps shade it from the sun, and prune one-third of its growth so that the leaves don't demand more than the roots can deliver. If you can, transplant only on an overcast or rainy day.

This prescription may fit into your daily routine, but my life is way too busy to reliably babysit all the transplanting I would like to do. So, I just make myself stop. I renounce transplanting until September.

It's hard to quit; I love rearranging the palette of the garden into pleasing color combinations.

The time to transplant a meditation practice into your life is now—in the spring or fall of your life. The summer of your life may be booked up, so transplanting then can require extra determination. And by the winter of your life—the conditions may be too tough. Coping with discomfort may be all consuming.

Plant, water, and feed your meditation practice now, while you can. Begin now, while the practice has time to establish a good root system, flourish, and produce some fruits (or vegetables!) of the spiritual life.

DISCONTENT IN THE GARDEN

I planted winter squash seeds yesterday—about three weeks too late, according to my reckoning. The soil was dusty-dry, and the afternoon had heated up to 88 degrees, so even the small effort of dragging a hoe through the clumpy, caked soil and pulling a few clods of field weeds drenched me with sweat.

This is one small vignette of discontent in the garden. I'm sure you could tell me your story, and then we'd commiserate with each other. Does this mean gardening is co-misery?

Listening to gardening conversations, you might wonder why people willingly put themselves through such dissatisfactions with bugs, plant diseases, and weather. And then the comparing mind (the only one we have) looks at the neighbor's garden and wonders why my beets are two inches tall and hers are a foot tall.

All this discontent doesn't stop us from getting dirt under our fingernails. We know in our hearts that joy and calm are lurking somewhere out there in the garden.

Pull the weeds of discontent—not by pulling ragweed, crabgrass, and lamb's quarters, but by simply relaxing into the garden as it is, without wishing for anything different. Contentment is a form of wishlessness, a place where our hearts can come to rest.

The mind is like Velcro for discontent and like Teflon for contentment. To overcome this "negativity bias," let's re-focus on the positive for 30 seconds, in order to start building new neural pathways that will enable us to fall more easily into contentment.

Start now. Look at a flower for 30 seconds. View your garden through a window from inside your house for 30 seconds. Stroll through your garden in the early morning or after dinner, and just relax.

SWORDS IN THE GARDEN

This past week, irises held the point of interest in the garden. Now they are fading. This is an excellent time to divide them, while I can still remember what color they are.

A garden designer refers to iris leaves and daylily leaves as "swords." How many swords do you want in your garden?

When you look at it that way, noticing shapes of leaves—you see that a smaller number looks better, more balanced with the other leaf shapes nearby.

A parable tells of a man shot by an arrow. His friend is a doctor and offers to pull out the arrow, but the man says, "Wait. Who shot the arrow? What village did he come from? Who are his relatives? What kind of wood was the arrow made of? What kind of feathers?" Then the man dies.

Imagine: We ourselves suffer a painful sensation, a painful emotion, a painful thought—like being shot by an arrow or impaled on a sword. Rather than extract the arrow or sword, we ruminate on it and thereby increase our suffering. Our sorrow, our heartache, can cease. All we have to do is pull out the first arrow.

How many swords do you want in the garden?

KEEPERS

Last night I used the last of my tomatillos to make salsa verde for a pork roast. Those tomatillos have been sitting in my basement for nine months—ever since I harvested them last September. Now that's what I call a keeper. No canning. No freezing. No special treatment. Just stored in a tray in a rack. *So* easy.

Spiritually, we keep five ethical precepts.

- we refrain from doing harm
- we refrain from taking what is not offered
- we refrain from sexual misconduct
- we refrain from speaking harshly or falsely
- we refrain from intoxicants

By keeping these five precepts, we build a base for happiness. The precepts aid our mindfulness, helping to hold the mind relatively clear of unskillful detritus. Doing no harm leads to less guilt and shame. Not taking what isn't offered leads to less bother from our conscience. Refraining from sexual misconduct leads to less heartbreak and more trusting relationships. Avoiding harsh or false speech leads to less regret. Refraining from intoxicants causes less poor judgment.

The precepts keep us safe and happy. They're keepers!

REPLANTING GOOD INTENTIONS

I'm doing a second planting of beets and chard. If I could figure out where to put them, I'd do a second planting of bush beans, because the bean plants exhaust themselves by early August, and it would be nice to have a fresh supply of green beans about then.

I made a "commit-to-sit" pledge with two friends I met recently on retreat. We committed to sitting two hours a day. This is proving to be fairly easy for one woman, and nearly impossible for the other, who just took an all-consuming summer teaching job. I myself wax and wane wildly, depending on whether I sit for an hour before the birds start singing at dawn.

It's time for me to replant my intention. This might mean going to bed earlier. Someone recently told me that the hours you sleep before midnight count double. I'll plant myself in bed before 10:00 tonight.

photo credit: ansonsaw / iStock

ALL BALLED UP

Seven years ago, I bought three six-inch-tall PJM rhododendrons and put them in my holding bed. I transplanted one, one died, and the third has limped along, looking quite puny.

Recently, I found that puny one yanked out (by a deer?) and lying on the ground. No wonder the small-leaved rhododendron was still only six inches tall. Its roots were growing in a circle, as if it were still confined to a three-inch pot.

Sometimes we confine ourselves—our emotions, our activities—to a very small space. Perhaps we were trained by authoritarian parents or teachers, or maybe we suffered a trauma that caused us to contract. Our own "rootball" may be confined to a very small space. Notice how contraction feels in the body. The mind may believe it's safer to stay small and fly under the radar. Question that belief.

Life is calling you.

SPECTACULAR FIREFLIES

The fireflies this year are spectacular.

My sweetie and I lie in the hammock for 20 minutes before bedtime and watch these "shooting stars" streak across the dark lawn. They are twinkling to the female glowworms who are lying in the grass. We rapidly turn our flashlight on and off just once— and watch the yard light up like Christmas as the ladies all turn on their lights for us.

This relaxation and en-joy-ment stimulates the rest-and-digest function of the parasympathetic nervous system, which is a good antidote to stress.

When you're stressed, where do you find refuge? Many people find solace outdoors in nature or with their pets. What's the place, person, or situation that causes you to feel safe and secure? Go there—in your mind—now.

Take a break and practice "natural" meditation.

photo credit: kororokerokero / iStock

A BEAR AND A PROBLEM

A black bear prowled around our house last evening, just before sunset. It smelled the birdfeeder on a second-story deck, in which we keep only a handful of seeds at a time. Fortunately, it did not climb up the ten feet to lick up a few stray sunflower seeds.

Inside the house, my sweetie was running from door to door, locking each one, and closing the garage door, which leads to the trash can where we store the birdseed. The trash can protects the seed from mice, but would be easy pickings for a bear.

Sometimes your mind is grappling with a "bear" of a problem that prowls around your mind, ravenously hungry, and looking for any excuse to justify our words or actions. The "I" wants to be right, and it will toss and turn the body for hours in the middle of the night to prove its point, over and over again.

The visit from the bear encourages me to clean up my act: (1) don't feed the birds in the summer, and (2) *no* meat scraps in the compost.

How do we clean up our minds? We can start by practicing compassion for ourselves and for the "bear" of a problem. First, we practice kindness toward ourselves and then, if we can, toward the other person. We notice what truth feels like: there's a relaxation that goes with truth. "Ahhh. Yes."

Chances are, the bear-of-a-problem has to repeat itself over and over, in our minds, telling us again and again and asking us to believe it time and time again. (Is that the definition of propaganda?) We only need to hear truth once to "know" it's true.

When you stand—or sit—on the side of truth, the mind relaxes and becomes like a still forest pool. As the Thai Forest meditation master Achaan Chah says, "All kinds of wild animals will come to drink there." Even a black bear.

THE HONOR SYSTEM

A nearby farmer loaded 26 bales of mulch hay onto my Toyota Tacoma pick-up truck. Wow! That Bonnie really knows how to stack hay! She did this while she was milking her five sweet brown Jersey cows. Every Monday, I pick up a half gallon of raw milk from her. While I'm there, I may buy a dozen eggs, a pound of butter, or some cream. It's all stored in a refrigerator, along with a cash box, in a tiny shed—so I can go there any time of the day or night. Everyone pays on the honor system.

If you look closely, you can see that we all depend on the honor system. Some 99.9 percent of our interpersonal transactions are indeed honorable. We don't take what isn't freely offered. We pay our share.

We *feel* right when we *do* the right thing, when we act honorably. When we act dishonorably, however, our conscience bothers us. We may dismiss a little cheat with a shrug of the shoulders, and think, "They'll never notice." But *we* notice. No one else may ever judge us for that little cheat. But if we were dying a few hours later, would we feel we were absolved? Or would we feel regret and remorse?

Acting honorably puts our minds at ease and leads to a sense of safety, even among all the strangers we see every day. By being trustworthy ourselves, we allow all the people around us—both friends and strangers—to experience some ease, as well.

VOLES 30. CHERYL 6.

Okay. The voles win. They have scored more of my three-inch broccoli seedlings than I have. Nibbled off at the stem.

Voles are quick, dark, gerbil-sized creatures that look like shadows darting through the Swiss chard, which they have also nibbled to the nubbins.

And in the game of cabbages, it's Voles 12, Cheryl 0. My little cabbage seedlings have completely disappeared, even the four six-inch seedlings of red cabbage that I bought at a farm stand.

I'm going to the Farmers' Market to buy six-packs of broccoli, green cabbage, red cabbage, and while I'm at it, Brussels sprouts. I want those muscular ten-inch-tall plants, so that a vole will need a chainsaw to cut down a broccoli tree.

A fellow Master Gardener has made several Vol-inators: He covers a little wooden Clementine box with bark to make it look like a burrow, but he furnishes it with mousetraps.

I just cannot do it. Every morning I take a vow not to harm creatures. I guess this includes the team of voles eating their way through my garden. I'd rather feed the voles my entire crop of cabbage.

But I do have a new strategy for our game next season.

CROAKING FROG

A single bullfrog croaks once every five or ten seconds all night long. Is he snoring? Is he tick-tocking to a very slow Nature's clock? Is he serenading his lady friend? Or talking in his sleep?

When someone dies, we say, "He croaked." Supposedly the death rattle sounds like croaking, but that must be a different species of frog from the tenor frog I'm hearing.

Perhaps this croaking frog is reminding me to reflect on death every day (and night). Life is short. Life is precious. Life is fleeting. And then it's gone.

The frog croaks.

photo credit: ca2hill / iStock

MOSQUITO REPELLENT FROM THAILAND

We went to Thailand three years ago, and one of the things I brought home as a souvenir was mosquito repellent. I figured that if any people knew how to deal with mosquitoes, it would be those who live in a tropical country that endures monsoons for three months and flooding for another three. I couldn't read the label, which bears a picture of lemon grass, but the spray bottle and the citronella scent appealed to me.

In May and June, I close my eyes and spray around my hairline, which is where the tiny blackflies like to bite me. Now that deer ticks are rampant, I also spray my cuffs at my wrists and ankles.

Mindfulness has the effect of repelling bothersome thoughts. Sure, you can still hear them buzzing around, and they may even land for a while. But soon they take off of their own accord without you swatting them.

Who knows? Maybe they're on their way to bother someone else.

GLADIOLUS STRESS

Our Farmers' Market sets up near the community garden on Sunday afternoons. Each of the 30 little garden plots is different from its neighbors, and each one is beautiful. A narrow flowerbed separates the garden from a wide swath of grass where the Farmers' Market takes place.

Last Sunday, I was sitting on the grass, eating dim sum, and enjoying my eye-level view of coreopsis and peonies, when Gladys rushed over and tried to prop up a broken gladiolus.

"Why can't people control their children?" she muttered. Then, seeing me, she said, "The world needs more meditation."

In fact, we can't control our children. We can't control our minds. And we can't control the world. Wanting control leads only to stress and distress.

We want to plant a gladiolus and see it flower. But some of them won't. We can't control the gladiolus. Nor can we control the children or the dogs, who walk over the flowers.

We can only watch the world unfold, constantly changing, according to its nature and *not* according to our wishes.

This is what's happening. Right now. Life.

SUMMER SOLSTICE BONFIRE

I bought an organic chicken at the Farmers' Market and boiled it to make chicken soup and chicken salad. But what to do with the skin and bones? You're not supposed to compost them, so as not to attract animals. But I'll tell you a secret: My compost is full of chicken bones and spare ribs.

In the winter, I cremate the bones in my wood stove. Now that it's the summer solstice, I'll have to have a bone-fire. Yes, that's where the word bonfire comes from—burning bones to make lime to sweeten the soil.

For eons, bonfires served as beacons, guiding distant travelers, on both land and sea. The beacon of our spiritual path guides us toward wisdom and compassion.

I'll be celebrating the summer solstice with a bonfire, rejoicing in the season's long days, when the light lasts nearly until bedtime, and relishing the warm nights.

photo credit: Miglena_Chordova / iStock

THE LONG VIEW

I attended a garden party on Sunday afternoon. The view was spectacular. From a large terrace, where we sat, we could see forty miles to the east, across the Connecticut River Valley and on to New Hampshire's southernmost mountain, Mount Monadnock, which stands alone, high above the rolling forested hills.

The long view settles us, calms us. Then our focus reverts to the people sitting near us, and the conversation narrows our attention on something near, and perhaps dear. Maybe the topic pricks us ever so slightly—family or local politics—or fluffs up our ego—family or our accomplishments or one of our opinions that we are sure is correct.

The long view is the quality of equanimity that underlies our practice, the ocean of space that surrounds us. Of course, our attention focuses on some *thing* near, some *thing* recognizable, some *thing* that feeds our sense of self.

Yet, if we step back and take the long view, we see that even these small things are held in spaciousness.

A SINGLE NIGHT

The night-blooming cereus flowered last night. Its petals began opening at dusk, and by dark the white flower was releasing its perfume to attract nectar-feeding bats and certain moths. By dawn the flower had wilted, drooping forlornly.

It's a short life for this remarkable nocturnal flower. I keep the straggly succulent as a houseplant all year long, just for this single night. Thank goodness, I was home at the right time!

Our own bloom time is less than a single century. Seventy, 80, 90, 100 years sounds like a long time when you are five or 20 or even 30, but then various parts of the body start to wilt and droop—breasts, bellies, various muscles. The first wrinkle appears.

Oh, we are so beautiful. And then a new day dawns.

photo credit: Gary Alvis / iStock

THE TIRE RETAINING WALL

When I moved into my house 31 years ago, I had more energy and time than I had money, so I built a retaining wall out of tires to hold back my east hillside. Tires? Over the years, they have been covered by creeping thyme and, more recently, sedum.

Yesterday I started taking apart the wall of tires to make way for one of stone. But change comes hard for the other person in my household. "If it ain't broke, don't fix it," he says.

To me, however, the tire wall looks sloppy, especially when examined closely. I look ahead to the time when our aging bodies will need to move out of a three-story house and into a single- level one. I do think a stone retaining wall will sell better than a tire wall. It's time to change the tires.

The garden changes from day to day. That east hillside flowerbed is now bare earth, and the retaining wall is being dismantled so that a reconstruction can begin. Change.

And after wrestling sand-filled tires out of the dirt for a couple of hours, and bouncing the sand out of them, I am tire-d!

STRAWBERRY SHORTCAKE

It's strawberry season here in the North Country, and on Saturday night we went to a strawberry shortcake dinner at the nearby church. The summer menu of potato salad, macaroni salad, cole slaw, and cold ham was just a prelude to the main attraction: shortcake with layers of sweet, luscious strawberries and whipped cream, with more cream dolloped generously on top.

Each table of eight was served family-style with a platter of strawberry-layered shortcake. The server cut the confection into eight pieces before our eyes, while an electric beater whirring in the background whipped up more cream for the construction that would go to another table of eight.

Strawberries: pleasant. Whipped cream: pleasant. Shortcake: pleasant. (Believe you me, the church women have this recipe perfected!)

I savored each pleasant bite, and then poured strawberry drippings from the empty platter on top of my remaining shortcake, watching as the confection turned from a buttercream color to pink-red. Pleasant. Pleasant. Pleasant. And then, even though more remained on my plate, suddenly the dessert felt unpleasant. It was too much.

I picked out the three remaining strawberries and popped them into my mouth: pleasant to the tongue, but unpleasant to the stomach. A soggy pink tennis-ball-sized piece of shortcake remained on my plate: unpleasant.

Pleasant becomes unpleasant. Amazing, isn't it? Five minutes ago, we thought our happiness depended on strawberry shortcake. Now that self-same dessert makes us unhappy.

Where *does* happiness truly reside?

Maybe we'll go pick a flat of strawberries this afternoon.

RUSSIAN RED KALE

Russian red kale has volunteered in the vegetable garden again, and it looks much stronger than the Russian red that I started from seed, which is about salad/mesclun size. Now I have twice the amount of kale I expected.

Last spring, the Russian kale sprouted tender young leaves on the thick brown stalks of the previous year, stalks I had not pulled out of the garden. I kept cutting the tender kale, which became larger as the summer progressed, eventually flowering and going to seed. This spring, I was surprised to find kale growing in my onion patch and 20 feet away, in the cucumber patch.

No matter what age we are, we can harvest the fruits (or vegetables) of our meditation practice. Our practice can grow lovely, delicious, small insights (e.g., "I'm going to hold my tongue for a minute right now"). Our practice can also sustain us. And occasionally we may find new, unexpected insights sprouting in our lives.

In these ways, we harvest our practice. The people around us benefit from our moments of calm amid the tempests of daily life.

REFRESHING THE FRONT STEP

This summer, my front step is overflowing with flowerpots. I've found a discount store where I can buy big glazed ceramic pots from Vietnam for $15 to $25 each. I bring the potted plants indoors in September, and because about 70 percent of them survive the winter in my solarium, I now have quite a collection of colorful plants.

Still, it's time to refurbish the two pansy pots. They looked good in April, but July is too hot for cool-weather pansies. So, I've been tucking various colorful leaves, and even another flower or two, into the pansy pots. Pulling out live flowers goes against my grain, but the pansies are leggy, wilty, and blooming sporadically. I want the flowers at the front door to look happy and welcoming.

Like the pansies, we, too, wilt and fail to flower when we are stressed. A friend with an intense summer job sometimes goes to bed at 7:30 in the evening in order to refresh herself. Her intention to meditate daily seems to have become lost in the daily crush of work. Ironically, she took this summer job so that she could afford to go on a month-long retreat next February. She will be pulling herself out of this stressful job come September.

What are your stressors? What stressful situations are you in right now? Is there some situation or some relationship that you can pull yourself out of? Maybe it's as "simple" as noticing a stressful thought and letting it go.

Let go. Let go of stress. Relax into summer. Relax into your garden.

WATERMELON POPPIES

The opium poppies (*Papaver somniflorum*) that I sowed in the snow in March are blooming now. I walk outside in the early morning to cut their watermelon-colored flowers. Each of a poppy's four petals has a purple cheek, so the cut flowers combine stunningly with the campanula growing nearby, as well as with the airy coral bells.

I arrange my bouquet indoors and set it on the kitchen table where I can look at it frequently.

Tomorrow afternoon, sometime between 2:00 and 4:00, all the petals will suddenly drop, leaving nude seed pods standing in the vase and a ruffled skirt of coral petals cast carelessly on the table.

Such is the ephemeralness of beauty.

photo credit: yamatao / iStock

IT'S A GOOD YEAR FOR WEEDS

"It's a good year for weeds," Sarah says, when I walk into my weekly writing group. Isn't every year a good year for weeds?

At the beginning of June, we have the illusion that our gardens are under control. My control. Ha! By the beginning of July, everything, and I mean *everything,* is growing fast. I weed one day, and the next day, more weeds have sprouted in that very spot that was bare the day before.

Mulch is the #1 weed control. I layer it on the flower beds in April, so there are no weeds to speak of there. In the vegetable garden, my only hope is that the weeds hide the vegetable plants from the voles. Too much weeding, and there's nothing left but veggie plants a.k.a. vole food.

Weedy thoughts and weedy behaviors abound in our daily lives. Yesterday morning, I was drawn into chitchat—talking about people. It's so enticing; it's so fun; it's so useless.

Or how about the nettles I exhibit toward my sweetie when he disagrees with me?

It's time to mulch with mindfulness.

THE SOLITUDE OF THE GARDEN

Not long ago, I attended a gardening symposium and happened to sit beside Anne Squires, a Master Gardener, who lives at the other end of the state.

"Did you come with a friend?" I asked.

"Oh, no, I came by myself," she said. "I love the solitude of the garden, and I think gardeners are more able to do things by themselves. Some of my friends don't go anywhere by themselves."

It's true that not everyone loves solitude, but the garden is a perfect place for those of us who need to get away from it all—even if that's only for a few minutes. Solitude—or the garden—is a fine place to listen to the still, small voice of our heart.

If we wait until we have company, we may find ourselves delaying our heart's desire for a long time—even a lifetime.

What do our hearts desire? Peace, happiness, freedom from suffering. What, specifically, does your tender heart desire? Contemplate this while you are tending the garden today.

BEAUTIFUL SONGS

Sitting on the deck this morning, I listen to birds singing. My forester neighbor, Lynn Levine, tells me how to distinguish between the song of a wood thrush and that of a hermit thrush. The hermit's song begins with a solitary note before moving on to a complicated and then melancholy flute trill. The wood thrush sings, "Ee-oh-lay."

We also distinguish among beautiful states of mind—loving-kindness, compassion, appreciative joy—in order to become more familiar with them. Loving-kindness is the heart's natural response to another person. Think of three-year-olds at a park. They immediately make friends with one another, without even knowing each other's name.

Compassion is the heart's natural response to suffering. Think of one-year-olds, who start crying when they hear another child crying.

We all still have these natural openings of the heart, these heavenly emotions, but often our beliefs clog their expression. "Big girls don't cry."

It's time to listen closely to our hearts, to hear these songs of love. There's no better place to hear these quiet songs than in the calm of our gardens.

GIVING AND ITS UNSEEN STRINGS

The last two 90-degree days brought breezes with them and gave us the delightful treat of hot and cool at the same time. Breezes blowing through open windows felt delightful in the meditation hall.

One woman brought a bouquet of flowers for the visiting nun who was leading the meditation and teaching. Another meditator quietly moved the bouquet to the anteroom, due to flower allergies.

How do you feel when your act of generosity is not accepted?

Perhaps you offer something and the recipient says, "No, thanks."

Or perhaps they accept, but don't put your gift in a place of honor (as with the flowers at the meditation hall). Or perhaps they accept, but then pass the gift on to someone else.

These are all opportunities to look at our intentions. Ostensibly, we thought we were being generous. But then we see/feel the strings we had unknowingly attached to our gift.

We want the recipients to be happy or grateful or surprised. Or we want them to like us or love us. Maybe we want them to think well of us. But perhaps they are less than grateful, considering our gift useless, ugly, or even a burden.

Like the road to hell, the road to stress and distress is paved with good intentions.

Let's be kind to ourselves. Let's give because we *want* to give, rather than focusing on how a recipient responds.

APPRECIATIVE JOY

I'm crawling around the vegetable garden on my hands and knees so that I can get a better look at a little brown bird that is sitting on top of a fencepost and singing his heart out to the four directions. Miraculously, he sits and sings till I'm crouching among the bush beans close enough to gaze at him.

He stops singing and preens himself unself-consciously, spreading his wing feathers. Then he just sits and watches. I hear the hum of bees, and see one rolling around in a nearby poppy. Gnat-size blackflies hover near my face. I hear the zoom of a hummingbird nearby.

I say the new Appreciative Joy phrases I learned at a recent meditation retreat.

How wonderful you are in your being.
I delight that you are here.

This seemingly nondescript little brown bird *is* wonderful. My heart swells, drinking in the summer late afternoon. Then the plain brown bird puffs out his breast and sings to the west. He hops around and sings to the east. Each in our own way, we are suffusing our world with joy.

POLLINATING OUR MEDITATION PRACTICE

Opium poppies (*Papaver somniflorum*) continue to bloom magnificently. I cut a bucketful every morning. When I arrive at the cutting bed, dozens of honeybees are buzzing around the flowers and rolling around in the watermelon-colored poppies. These flowers are so beautiful, I'd roll around in them too, if I could.

How do we pollinate our meditation practice? If we want it to bear fruit, then we need to study and practice.

"Study" may be as simple as reading this book, or another that inspires you. Or you may want to download a dharma talk and listen to it, in the car on the way to work or while you prepare dinner.

Practice includes daily sitting, and, if possible, a regular meditation session with other people. Also, if you can, plan an annual meditation retreat of at least seven days. (I commit to a month-long retreat and four five-day retreats every year.)

Likewise critical is the practice of wholesome qualities such as patience, generosity, and kindness. Pollinating these flowers helps us bloom where we are planted.

WEEDING AND WEEPING

My dental hygienist, Martha, tells me she bought a new house. She wasn't going to do any gardening, what with all the moving and settling in. The yard was rocky, except for one square patch of dirt. So, she quickly planted some tomatoes, some squash, and some lettuce. Then one month ago today, her aging mother died unexpectedly.

"I've spent so much time out there weeding," she says.

"Weeding and weeping?" I ask.

"Well, you think things over when you're in the garden," she replies. "Really, that garden is a godsend. I don't know what I would have done without it."

Our gardens are wonderful places for contemplation as we grapple with the sadnesses, losses, and yes, the joys of life.

Choose a contemplation from this collection or another dharma book and carry it out to the garden today.

photo credit: stock_colors / iStock

OUTER AND INNER CLIMATE

I am fortunate to have my own well that produces 12 gallons of water a minute—so, on these sweltering days, the only cost of watering the gardens for hours and hours is the cost of electricity.

And on such sunny days, my electricity is "free," as it comes from solar-voltaics, which is to say, the sun.

Friends who live in town have utilized a brook running around the back of their property. They put a little pump in the brook, attached it to a hose, and water their gardens from the brook in order to avoid a startlingly high water bill.

The combination of sun, water, and rich earth means the plants in the veggie garden are growing by leaps and bounds.

In the 95-degree afternoons, I drive to nearby ponds or rivers to immerse myself for relief from the sun's heat. Ahhh. Cool water refreshes the body.

When our inner climate heats up with irritation or desire, how do we cool ourselves down? Mindfulness is the cool water that refreshes our senses.

Yes, we may still have to suffer a bit with the inner heat of "I can't believe they...." or "I want...." Feel where those thoughts reside in your body.

Put your attention on those sensations as if on an acupressure point.

Hold your attention on that tender spot. Hold it. Hold it. Tears may come to your eyes. This is the water that cools down the inner climate.

THE PROLIFERATION OF MINT

Mint is such a tasty herb, but how many people have I warned: "Don't plant it!"

Mint is a spreader par excellence. When I started my herb garden, I wanted every kind of mint. But then I found that I used very few varieties. I actually prefer apple mint, identifiable by its fuzzy leaf, which I use to make iced tea. Someone gave me chocolate mint, and that's a nice addition, but the apple mint has overrun it.

My method of keeping the mint patch under control is to make mint iced tea every day. On these hot days, I "pick" mint in the afternoon, which is to say I pull it up by as much root as I can, and clip off the root. When I have a big handful of stems, I rinse them under the faucet and stuff them into a half-gallon glass pitcher, add boiling water, and let it cool.

The pitcher goes into the refrigerator by evening, and the next day, we have cold mint tea all day long to cool and refresh us.

Just as mint unchecked will overrun our gardens, the hindrances—sense desire, ill-will, sleepiness, anxiety, and doubt—will overrun our lives, if we do not restrain them. One way to hold them back is by applying mindfulness to our daily life. One by one, we pull back on desiring, expressing a zinger, collapsing, worrying, or doubting. We take a close look at the presenting circumstance, and in this way, we clip the root of that momentary hindrance.

We ourselves are refreshed and able to relax into the next moment, maybe with a glass of cold mint tea in hand.

ALLERGIC TO MINDFULNESS

My sweetie has been taking a spoonful of local bee pollen every day since March in an effort to alleviate his summer allergies. So far, it's working. He doesn't really like the taste of the bee pollen, which he chases down with a glass of fruit juice.

I have to confess that for many years, decades even, I was allergic to mindfulness. On the one hand, I could see that it was good medicine for the ills of daily life, but as long as I was feeling good, mindfulness seemed, well, *so* boring.

Besides, I loved the way my mind worked. My particular mind is very good at problem-solving, and its form of creativity gives insights into how people and the world behave. Oh! How I love that playground. Why rein in the mind? Why limit it in the bounds of mindfulness? Letting the mind run free is so much more fun and interesting.

My know-it-all mind looked at the breath once and thought it knew all about the breath. My know-it-all mind did walking meditation once and then became bored. My know-it-all mind thought it knew everything. Yeah, yeah, yeah.

Then a teacher introduced me to contemplations, and my meditation practice bloomed. Contemplations on aging, illness, and death interest my mind, but the way to get to the contemplations is to walk down the path of mindfulness and first calm the mind so that it can look deeply into these difficult subjects. Mindfulness is the key that opens the gate to the secret garden of Life, so that we can see things as they really are.

BEGINNER'S MIND

While I was at the meditation center last week, one of the staff, Kristy, dug up a patch of irises and daylilies and replanted them along a stone wall. I'd stopped transplanting because of the heat, which can be tough on plants, but Kristy was undeterred.

I went in to the 7 P.M. meditation, and she was digging. Forty-five minutes later, when I walked out, she was heavily watering the new bed.

This is a great example of "beginner's mind." Kristy had intention; she applied effort; she got results. The expert (me) wouldn't have applied the effort, because the expert "knows too much."

Sometimes, we think that by transplanting the expert's knowledge/opinion into our own experience, we'll reduce our stress of not-knowing. That can be true. But we might also reduce our happiness.

Kristy looked pretty happy about the new flowerbed. And I've been waiting for years for someone to do something with that overgrown patch of daylilies and irises, so I was happy too.

GLAD FOR GLADS

Gladioli are blooming, and I am glad. I love my glads. I made a commitment to gladioli about a dozen years ago: they are the only annual bulb (corm, actually) that I am willing to plant in the spring, dig up in the fall, and store during the winter.

Gladioli start blooming in mid-July and flower though the end of August. Like daffodils, gladioli have early-season varieties as well as mid-season and late-season ones.

Gladness is one of the divine emotions, closely related to loving-kindness. Feeling glad to see a friend is a shout-out of love.

I'm glad to see my old friends, the gladioli.

photo credit: User10095428_393 / iStock

STICKINESS

Lately southern Vermont has felt and smelled like the tropics. With all the rain, we've been enveloped in a warm fog every morning, as the moisture slowly evaporates into the 87-percent-humid air. As the day's temperature increases, the humidity decreases—until the next thunderstorm, which usually occurs in the afternoon.

Doors and windows swell and stick. With the slightest exertion, I feel sticky, too.

When thoughts stick to us, that's a clue that we are feeling stress. This is what stickiness feels like: inescapable, no way out.

Air-condition your mind by accepting what is. Ask yourself: *Is this thought any of my business? Or is it someone else's?* Even if a thought seems to be about "me" and "mine," it might be none of our business. Maybe we just have to wait for outer events and conditions to unfold.

Notice what a sticky mind feels like in the body. Notice where it "rubs" and "grabs" the body. Then notice that the sticky thought is a thought. It's just a thought. And you can't hold onto that thought no matter how hard you try.

The door opens on the next thought.

GOING TO SEED

Shall I let flowers go to seed? Or should I deadhead them right away?

I am an inveterate starter of seeds, and as a result, my flowerbeds look unkempt. I recently cut the lupine stalks and spread their black seeds in a bed of wood chips. Columbine seeds are ripening, and I'm already thinking about next year's columbine crop. All of May's beautiful money plant is now faded and browning, but it has yet to become silvery with age.

Last evening, I toured a handsome and remarkably tidy July garden. I came home to my own less orderly flowerbeds: some are enjoying glorious blooms, while others are straggly. The overall effect: it appears as though way too many things are happening at the same time.

Shall I perpetuate the illusion of agelessness and allow only blooming flowers? Or can I let my flowerbeds reflect all of life—human, animal, and plant—which will eventually go to seed?

VITAMINS FOR TOMATOES

I have two buckets of manure tea in the vegetable garden.

"Manure tea?" Visitors to my garden wrinkle their noses, as if this tea is a medicine they should take.

"For the tomatoes," I explain, and their faces relax.

"Oh," they say, exhaling with relief.

I make manure tea by filling a bucket one-third full of manure, then topping it off with water and letting it steep for several days. After "watering" the plants, I refill the bucket with water again.

The tomato plants don't tell me how manure tea tastes, but the adolescent plants are just beginning to yield tiny fruits, and they are bursting out of their four-foot-tall cages. I'm guessing the dose of liquid vitamins works.

We take our daily vitamins, too, to keep our bodies strong. A daily dose of meditation (Vitamin M) has a positive effect on our daily life. There's Vitamin C (for calm) and Vitamin H (for happiness). Maybe you notice the effect of vitamin A- (for anxiety reduction). I especially like the effect of Vitamin I- because it reduces my irritation, particularly towards the person with whom I live.

Let's fertilize our positive qualities by taking a dose of mindfulness every day.

HARVESTING TOMATOES—AND MINDFULNESS

I picked my first Sun Gold cherry tomato today. Delicious!

Popping one of these yellow-orange babies into your mouth is an unforgettable rite of summer. The tomato tastes and smells like summer. This is the reason I planted those tiny seeds five months ago.

Every time we practice mindfulness in our daily lives, we are planting a tiny seed. Sometimes, like that one-sixteenth-inch-wide tomato seed, our mindfulness looks pathetically small compared to the avalanche of thoughts and feelings swirling around in our minds.

We keep that seed warm by adding kind-heartedness toward ourselves, and voila! Mindfulness sprouts two "leaves," and for two seconds we leave judgments and opinions aside and simply acknowledge the present moment.

We water mindfulness daily by paying attention to what we are doing/saying/thinking. Five months later, what was in that tiny tomato seed is four feet tall and three feet wide and producing a handful of tomatoes, each one filled with tiny, juicy seeds.

WEED? OR WILDFLOWER?

Queen Anne's Lace is abloom with its lacy white flowers. My sweetie, the mower, considers it a weed, despite its delicate blossoms. I remind him of the time we held hands and walked through a field of Queen Anne's Lace. Weed? Or wildflower?

How do we recognize the weeds/wildflowers in our daily lives? Stress is a clue. If we feel stress or distress, then that situation, that thought, is a weed. And if we feel divine—love, compassion, joy, gratitude, peace—then it's a wildflower.

My sweetie is a concert pianist—he attends two, three, or even four concerts every summer weekend. That feels too "weedy" to me; my limit is one concert per weekend. While my sweetie basks in divine music, I take a walk in a field of wildflowers.

photo credit: sallymidcoastmaine / iStock

THISTLE ROOTS

My friend Melissa spent three hours digging thistle roots out of her flowerbed. First, she dug down about a foot into clay, which she doesn't otherwise find in her garden. Then she followed the root, which can extend another seven feet.

Our unskillful habits are also deeply rooted. Rather than becoming dismayed by all these habits, choose just one to focus on and become acquainted with.

Lust? Impulse buying? Complaining? Impatience? Zinger opinions? Wishy-washiness?

Spend an hour, or two or three, noticing when the tendency arises. Don't just tug on it when it comes over you—that's like cutting down thistle. The results are temporary, and the root is still sprouting below ground. Instead, pay attention and become interested enough that you follow the root feeling. Notice how the habit feels in your body. Relax into that uncomfortable place.

Thistle is ouchy. Notice if you are "allergic" to the emotion behind the habit.

Rooting out unskillful tendencies takes patience. It also requires renouncing the path of least resistance. Neurons that fire together wire together, and our unskillful habits have laid down a well-worn neuronal pathway.

Beating up on yourself for an unskillful habit only lays down the tracks for beating up on yourself. What's the use of that?

Practice the kindness of mindfulness. With mindfulness, we attend to our garden, one weed at a time.

BIG BASIL AND LITTLE BASIL

The basil in my Herb-Flower-Vegetable Medley Garden is looking great. It's ready to harvest. Meanwhile, the same basil in the vegetable garden is only three inches tall.

I planted the basil in the two gardens on the same day and from the same six-pack. What accounts for the difference?

The Medley Garden is a brand-new garden just outside the back door. Last fall, I filled its beds with cow manure. The veggie garden didn't even get a dose of compost this year.

What kind of soil do you dwell in? Is your life producing an abundance of joy? Or stress? Or both?

Our habits of mind can give rise to complaining about the way things are and desiring something else. Or we can focus on feelings of kindness, joy, and gratitude. Where are you placing your attention?

I'm focusing on the great-looking basil out the back door. And yes, I'm going to give some attention to that pathetic basil in the vegetable garden. I'll water it with compost tea.

TO SQUASH? OR NOT TO SQUASH?

I just picked my first summer squash. I love these delicate yellow squashes sautéed in butter and fresh garlic with a dash of tamari.

The word "squash" comes from the Algonquin, in which the suffix *-ash* is the plural.

Plural is definitely the word to use when it comes to summer squash and zucchini. I prefer picking these squashes when they are only six inches long, as they are sweetest when small. But I love even the ones that get away, the ones I don't discover till they are a foot or two long. These I grate in the food processor and freeze in baggies to bake into blond brownies over the winter.

In meditation, we can watch the plural ways of our mind wandering off. We don't "squash" those thoughts. (Pun intended.) We simply recognize them; labeling is very effective here.

You can "pick" some thoughts while they are young and small, but others will get away from you and develop into great big stories. "Pick" those big thoughts by labeling them. Then settle in and watch the mind grow.

THE JULY GARDEN

Just when July flowers are peaking, two of my flowerbeds are solid green. I gaze longingly at other people's blooming gardens that shout *July!* I forget that my two green beds shouted *May!* and are now resting from their exertions. When the *July!* beds are resting in September, the now-green beds will be singing again.

I want flowers now. Want. Now. But now is an oven—too hot to launch any refurbishing of the green-on-green gardens. Want. Wanting things to be different than they are. This is the stress of gardening.

Could I let go and be content with what is? Green is a beautiful color (especially if you live in the desert), and my garden bears many shades of green.

BUG JOY

After strolling through the garden in my nightgown this morning, I came back indoors and felt something crawling on my leg. Even though the weather is too hot for ticks, I live in deer tick country, so I looked carefully. About twice the size of a wood tick, this six-legged insect looked like a beetle.

A baby lightning bug! About half an inch long, it spread its wings and flew away.

So that's the result of the flurry of fireflies in June. The males flying their flashers around, and the females lying in the grass glowing back.

Lightning bugs bring joy—to young children chasing them and to grown-ups lying in a hammock at 10 P.M. looking at the night sky full of stars and fireflies.

CHILDREN IN THE GARDEN

My grandchildren are coming to the garden this weekend, and I feel like Santa's elf. Or maybe the Easter Bunny's elf? I'm forgoing my own harvest for a couple of days, so the children can have the joy of finding cherry tomatoes! Green beans! Going out to the garden with children turns into a treasure hunt.

Eleven-year-old Chloe has been a serious cook for the past five years, so she will enjoy finding bok choy, kale, and the various greens such as mizuna and cress. We will probably pull an onion and some garlic for flavor. Max, aged seven, likes digging for the buried treasure of potatoes and carrots. Before Chloe and Max leave, we will pick bouquets of flowers that their mother can take home with her.

Sharing the garden and the joy of the garden is a form of generosity. The joy of giving from the garden is so easy. And it will circle right back into all of us when Chloe prepares the Saturday evening meal.

photo credit: NataliaLeb / iStock

SUN-DRYING TOMATOES
IN THE DEHYDRATOR YOU ALREADY OWN

Here comes the cherry tomato (Sun) Gold rush. And I've just heard of a great way to sun-dry those tomatoes—on the dashboard of the car. Yes. Park your car in the sun. Place the fruit or vegetables in a shallow box and put it on the dashboard on a sunny day.

Do you have some bad habits you'd like to dry up? Park those in the steady warmth of non-judgmental mindfulness. Notice what happens just before and just after the bad habit appears.

How does your mouth taste *after* the sweet goodie? *Really* feel/taste that. How does your body feel just before you open the refrigerator door? Really feel that.

No need for the mind to get involved with judging. Low-key mindfulness will have the insight. Don't work the mind harder; work smarter.

I feel joy at the thought of sun-dried tomatoes.

DIFFERENT GARDENING STYLES

When I go outdoors in the morning, I stroll around my flowerbeds, clippers in one hand, bucket in the other. I'm deadheading and propping up flowers, and generally tidying up some flowerbed or other.

At 7:45, I arrive for meditation at my neighbor Connie's, and there she is in her nightgown hauling foot-tall (or more!) weeds out of her vegetable gardens, her hands caked with dirt, and her white nightie pretty well smudged.

For me, flowers are the priority; for her, vegetables.

The mind loves to compare. So far as I can see, that's *all* the mind actually does. And in this comparison, the mind wants to divide the world into good and bad, black and white, better and worse. Yet here we are, Connie and I, two old friends with very different gardening interests and styles, both reaping joy.

DAY-LONG LILIES

Our friends who have a spectacular daylily garden come for dinner and bring a wicker basket filled with today's blooms. I try to name the colors—lemon-peel yellow, brick red, tangerine, plum, peach, cream.

After dinner, while we're talking in the living room, I rearrange the single flowers to see the effect of their colors. A petal comes loose.

"Eat it," says Frank.

Mmmm. Nice crisp texture with a slightly perfumy taste.

"Are they in water?" my sweetie asks with concern.

"No," says Claire. "They just last a day. Tomorrow morning they'll be compost."

I am of the nature to die. Death is unavoidable—for daylilies and for me. Death is certain for all of us, but unlike the daylilies with a one-day life span, my life span is unknown. The time of my death is uncertain.

As we talk about children and grandchildren, I continue to finger the daylilies. The triple peach has the sweetest fragrance. The grape-colored six-pointed star measures eight inches across, while its plum-colored cousin with recurved petals is demurely petite by comparison.

When Frank and Claire leave, I send their basket home with them and scatter the loose blossoms on the kitchen table. The floral funeral will come at dawn.

DEEP SUMMER

Deep summer has arrived. Cricket songs capture our attention. The temperature has been in the 90s for many more days than usual, and rivers, lakes, and ponds are now quite comfortable for swimming. Then, too, mid-summer means deep tans and ripe tomatoes.

The great tomato race begins. They spill off the kitchen window sill onto the counter. Red cherry tomatoes in a green bowl; Sun Golds in a blue bowl. We're eating tomatoes for all three meals and snacking on them, too. Salsa, BLTs, bruschetta, tomato and cucumber salads. The cucumbers are multiplying, as well, when our backs are turned! Now the garden is nearing full adulthood, and we're reaping its cornucopia.

We en-joy this stage of garden life when fresh vegetables are bountiful. Now is the time to feel deep gratitude for the abundance of our gardens—and spread the joy by giving the extras to friends or to a community food pantry.

photo credit: mucella / iStock

THE SUMMER SAG

I call this season the summer sag. I look at my flowerbeds, and all I see is green. Where are the flowers? They must be blooming in someone else's full-sun garden, because they are not blossoming here in partial shade.

I confess: I still haven't mastered the art of the rolling bloom—a little garden that is constantly flowering. Apparently, I'm in good company. When the Garden Club toured my garden last week, I sighed about this, and the president asked, "Who has mastered it?"

Those photos in gardening magazines and books are so beautiful. And the British make it sound so simple. "Just cut back the pulmonaria (or the doronicum or the….), and they will bloom again." They will bloom again in July if your summer high temperature is 70 degrees, but our weather on this side of the pond has been cooking for the past several weeks.

This is the delusion, whose spell we fall under: we can have a flower-filled garden like the ones in the photos. But the reality is, there are times in which the garden exhibits only greenery.

We live our lives in these sorts of hopeful delusions—that things will be different from what they are. We want more of the pleasant (flowers) and less of the unpleasant (plain greenery). We stay in constant motion, tweaking our environment—inner or outer. And we remain disappointed or disgusted.

We have an alternative. The first step is mindfulness. Let's begin here today by walking through our gardens and examining what is: noticing the pleasant and noticing the unpleasant.

The garden may sag, but our mindfulness doesn't need to.

FAREWELL TO MY SPADING FORK

While I was prying some brick-red daylilies out of the ground with my spading fork, the D-shaped handle broke off the wooden shaft. My best gardening friend for the past 29 years—the one that has given me many an aching back as well as so much joy—that friend's spine was now broken.

I took its mud-encrusted tines to Brown & Roberts—our locally-owned hardware store—and asked them to put on a new D-handle. The clerk shook his head and compared prices: a new fork cost $22.98, a new wooden shaft for my old fork cost $15.98. I watched him examining the bent tines, their metal polished to a dull gleam from grinding against numerous rocks. He then pronounced the death of my good friend who has spent every spring standing near the vegetable garden, calling me to come out and play.

Everything I cherish will change and vanish is the fourth of the Five Daily Buddhist Recollections. I placed my cherished friend next to the trash bag that's going to vanish into the dumpster tomorrow.

Farewell, my dear.

HOUSEWARMING AND HEARTWARMING

My step-daughter has moved into a new home in Boston, and the flowerbeds there have not been tended in decades. She asked me for some plants, which I will give her in the fall when the weather cools down enough for transplanting. For now, my housewarming present to her is a weeder and her grandmother's trowel, which I have been saving for her for nineteen years.

I'm looking forward to using that weeder and the trowel myself when I visit her in the fall with a few of her grandmother's plants.

We think of particular plants as having come from our grandmothers' or our friends' gardens, but when we look closely, we see that this is really just an idea. The actual leaves, the flowers, and sections of the roots, are different from those that flourished when our grandmothers gardened. That flower, which reminds us so sweetly of our good friend, is several generations removed from the actual plant she gave us years ago.

Nevertheless, we look at Granny's clematis, her lily-of-the-valley, and smile as we remember the person whom we loved.

TALL PLANT SEASON

Full summer is the season of tall plants blooming. Phlox, bee balm, and all manner of yellow sunflower-y-looking things. In April and May, the short ones bloom—little ground-cover-type things. Johnny-jump-ups and forget-me-nots. Some plants are so short that you may not at first even notice or recognize them—draba or mazus or arabis. Yet, what welcome patches of color they offer in early spring.

Now, after months of inching up, butterfly bush, eupatorium, and verbascum are taller than I am.

Meditation practice also varies from person to person. A few of us bloom early on. The rest grow and grow, inching along before flowering. Whatever our tendency, let us simply be content with growing in our practice, knowing that our spiritual life can also flower.

JAPANESE BEETLES

Japanese beetles are feasting on my zinnias and potatoes, creating leaf lacework. They copulate on a marriage bed of creamy white marigolds. The beetles themselves are beautiful—their iridescent blue-green and bronze bodies shimmering in July's hot sun.

One friend, Kai, goes out to her vegetable garden every morning and picks off the beetles. It's a "weeding" out of bugs—a preventative measure that protects the life of the plant.

This sort of steady attention is a quality we bring to meditation. Every day, we spend some time sitting quietly. At first, we simply notice the what's bugging our mind and identify them one by one: irritation, desire, confusion. Eventually we apply the antidotes: loving-kindness for irritation, generosity for desire, and wisdom for confusion.

A VERY SMALL GARDEN

The staff at the retreat center has a small vegetable and flower garden, about eight feet long and three feet wide. Two lawn chairs sit beside it, and that is where I go to make my daily phone call to my sweetie, since I'm not on a silent retreat.

There are two tomato plants, three poles for pole beans, a squash plant, about three feet of carrots, one basil plant, sunflowers, and roses. In other words, this very small garden needs very little tending. Yet it brings great happiness, not only to the people who planted it, but to the string of people who go out there, at a distance from the retreat center's main buildings, to call home every day.

Our formal meditation practice can be like this: a small patch in our busy workday, at a slight distance from the people and activities of our life. If we tend our small practice daily, the results will make us happy, and, after a short time, bear the fruit (or vegetables) of the spiritual life.

RELAX INTO AUGUST

August. Let's enjoy our flower gardens without fussing. We've worked hard to bring them along; let's sit back and delight in them.

Let's go out to the vegetable garden and harvest some tomatoes, beans, cucumbers, and squash. We'll pick the cucumbers and squash small and tender and sweet.

Then let life be. Just as it is. Let the gardens be—just as they are. Plop yourself down in nature, somewhere near a body of water—a lake, a pond, a river, a stream—or, if you can get there, the sea. Before you pick up a book or your smart phone, look around you. Relax. Relax into summer. Relax into the present moment.

photo credit: CribbVisuals / iStock

TRAINING POLE BEANS UP

My pole beans, like mischievous children, are running away, over the ground, instead of climbing their poles. I have to train them, one by one, to send their vines up, not out.

Our minds can also be quite mischievous at times, running here and there, getting into trouble, causing stress and distress. We sit down in meditation to train our minds to pay attention to the present moment. The mind runs hither and thither. We direct our attention back to our breath or to sensations of the body.

When we realize a moment of concentration, just a single moment in which the mind appears stable, we can look out over the forest of thoughts, and, perhaps, harvest a single insight.

Oh, that green bean is so fresh and delicious!

PICKING VITAMIN C

I caught a cold while I was on retreat, so, flying home, I kept drinking water and dozing. After I picked up my car, I drank a bottle of HonestTea and a can of seltzer water. By the time I reached the Vermont Welcome Center on Interstate 91, I was *really* ready for a bathroom break.

The Welcome Center is beautifully landscaped; the "islands" that separate the parking lot from the driveway were filled with *Rosa rugosa*, their ripe red fruits gleaming in the sun. I picked a handful on my way in, and another handful on my way out.

Rose hips are quite sweet. They are also extremely seedy. But I was desperate for Vitamin C, and those little seeds are good "intestinal brooms."

Do you take daily vitamins? Meditation is our Vitamin M. The prescription: Take one daily.

Yes, meditation can be a little seedy, and it can be a little bit sweet. But we all know, it's really good for you.

TOO MANY CHERRY TOMATOES

It's cherry tomato season. Even though I have tried to limit my plants—to three Sun Golds and two grape tomatoes—I still harvest dozens of these luscious little fruits every day. Then, too, I admit—at the last moment, at a plant sale supporting a youth program, I bought three more pale yellow "cherry" tomato plants whose fruits are the size of golf balls.

This is the price of desire, that little voice that says, "Oh, I'll just have one or two more." Three months later, what do you do with an abundant crop?

I could complain about it as if it's someone else's fault that I'm overwhelmed by little tomatoes. I could give away my extra cherry tomatoes and enjoy knowing someone else will en-joy them.

Here's what I actually do: I sun-dry the cherry tomatoes. Two racks of them are in the food dryer right now. My homemade food dryer is powered by four 100-watt light bulbs. You can "sun" dry tomatoes in a low oven (200 degrees) overnight, too, if you leave the oven door cracked.

You might call this approach making lemonade out of lemons. I tell you, those sun-dried tomato "chips" are sweet and tart. Mmmm.

PAY IT FORWARD

A meditation friend is coming this morning to cut flowers for her daughter's wedding. My flower garden might look bare tomorrow. Or I might not even be able to tell the difference.

Should I close my heart and my garden out of fear of the unknown? Shall I be closefisted (also called grasping)? Or shall I open my hand in friendliness and generosity? What would you do?

I could pay it forward—as opposed to paying back the innumerable kindnesses that have been done to me. Just last week, someone gave me three plants and two kinds of seed. I might or might not ever pay her back in plants, but I can pay the plants—or flowers—forward. Today.

photo credit: Natalia Bratslavsky / iStock

BURROWING

A groundhog has taken up residence ten feet away from my vegetable garden. I wish I lived ten feet away from *my* grocery store!

I can see the well-worn path from the burrow to the garden fence. I suppose the groundhog piglets go straight through the fence, even though the fence's holes are quite narrow.

My makeshift garden gate has been bent out of shape by parent groundhogs that easily burrow under it. I've lost all my beans, cucumbers, broccoli, cabbage, and Brussels sprouts to groundhogs and voles.

What burrows into our life and steals the fruit of our spiritual path?

Summer is wonderful for all the vacations and mini-vacations and company, but all the comings and goings of friends and family can impact our meditation practice.

We may not immediately notice the loss of the fruits of our meditation practice. What is it, specifically, that you lose when you don't meditate?

I lose an easy-going-ness. I become more irritable on days when I don't meditate. A friend who meditates to reduce her blood pressure loses her calmer blood pressure.

Now it's time to take another look at that groundhog burrow.

EIGHT KINDS OF BASIL

The basil looks great now, in the height of summer. Each plant has developed into a small bush.

In May, I managed to collect several varieties—ordinary sweet basil, purple basil, opal basil with mottled green and purple leaves, Thai basil, lemon basil, lime basil, cinnamon basil, and the small-leaved globe basil.

Now, of course, I can't keep up with all of this burgeoning basil. Pesto pasta for dinner one evening, Thai curry the next. What am I going to do with cinnamon basil?

All these basils are the fruits of desire. In May, I planted a dozen of each. Fortunately, I found only one cinnamon basil plant. Now I'm overwhelmed with the thought of harvesting all these basils.

This is what happens: We get what we ask for: we were so sure that this thing we wanted (basil, in my case) would make us happy. (And I am very happy to eat it.) But we didn't notice the underbelly of the object of our desire.

Notice it now. Feel the strain. Notice that it's a thought. Only a thought. It comes. It goes.

Let's go out to the garden and pick some basil.

REPLANTING OUR INTENTION

Some years ago, I collected seeds from a rare white mullein I spotted growing along the roadside. This mullein is quite different from the common roadside plant with fuzzy gray leaves and a five- to seven-foot-tall stalk of very small yellow flowers.

This white-blooming variety must have escaped from a nursery, now defunct, and reseeded itself on the nearby roadside. When it blooms in early July, the stalk is covered with stunning two-inch-wide white flowers.

I collected seed for three or four years before one finally took hold in my garden. Now I have dozens of these splendid white mullein volunteering in my sunny beds.

We have to replant our intention quite frequently, even during a single period of meditation. We replant the intention to be mindful, to be kind, or to practice patience. Then, one day, mindfulness or kindness or patience shows up in a place where we didn't expect it, and we en-joy the blooming of our practice.

PLAN FOR FALL PLANTING. NOW.

Now is the time to plant the fall garden: broccoli, chard, kale, bok choy, and lettuces prefer cool weather. As the hot-season crops—the cucumbers, tomatoes, peppers, and eggplants—begin to look peaked with the first chill in the air, the cool-weather vegetables begin to flex their muscles.

Now, in the height of your own summer strength and health, is the time to plant the crop that will reward you when you begin to feel a bit peaked in the fall of your life.

What will you do when the body becomes as spotted as an old tomato plant? When your bones begin to look as hole-y as slug-chewed greens? The material world, including our bodies, ages and decays.

Plant your spiritual practice now, so that you can begin to reap the fruits of the spiritual life.

This daily foray into quiet reminds us of what is most important in our lives.

Take a moment now. Right now. Close your eyes and listen. Close your eyes and feel the body. Close your eyes and notice your breath.

Nourish yourself with the daily sustenance of natural food and natural meditation.

THE FALL-ING GARDEN

A misting rain fell this morning—perfect for our too-dry gardens that are limping into late summer. My body has the same sunburned, dried-out, curled-at-the edges look as the fading leaves of Solomon's seal.

The phlox and peegee hydrangea are just entering their heyday. The tall purple ironweed (*Vernonia altissima*) reigns supreme.

This is the time of year when many gardeners throw up their hands. "I've had it," they say. But some few of us are dedicated to enjoying the autumn of our lives. I've been cultivating a fall garden for some years, so for the next month, I'll have more and more blooms.

"Where do you get your energy?" my step-daughter recently asked.

Whether it's grandchildren, flowers, or life, I guess the answer is: Love.

I often think of this teaching of the Buddha:

This existence of ours is as transient as autumn clouds.
To watch the birth and death of beings is like looking at the movements of a dance.
A lifetime is like a flash of lightning in the sky,
rushing by, like a torrent down a steep mountain.

WHEN LIFE FEELS SANDY

When my house was built, truckloads of gravelly sand were brought in to backfill around the foundation. Since the house stands on a slope, I have a daylight basement; the basement door opens beside a hill of sandy gravel that is well shaded by the cantilevered solarium above.

For years I despaired over this sand pile that seemed to collect odds and ends and look generally disreputable. Then a few years ago, with a devil-may-care attitude, I planted a six-pack of begonias there. They flourished! The next year, I added impatiens and pink polka-dot plant. Now two varieties of bleeding hearts have volunteered to grow in this totally shaded, incorrigibly dry spot.

No matter how bleak our lives or meditation practice may look, a little creativity can suddenly enliven things, creating a spot of interest. This interested attitude in turn creates the energy for us to continue gardening—or meditating.

photo credit: ChanwitOhm / iStock

HUMMINGBIRD JOY

On these summer mornings, I sit on my second-story deck to do my meditation. From here I have a great view of my lawn and gardens. A few years ago, we refurbished the deck and replaced the two-board sides with two wires. The plastic-coated wire doesn't interrupt the view of the garden as the boards did, and the wires do give a feeling of enclosure.

This morning, a hummingbird perched on a wire about four feet in front of me. He appeared to be a juvenile, because his feathers were still mottled. His ruby throat was a bit patchy. And his beak was only an inch long.

Hummingbirds like to perch on bare (i.e., dead) branches—I guess that gives them the best view—and this morning the plastic-coated wire served the same purpose. I watched his tail move slightly up and down as if he were learning to balance. He cocked his head this way and that—one eye looking up at the sky, checking for danger. A chickadee landed nearby, but the baby boy hummingbird wasn't threatened.

Watching birds brings me a lot of joy. This joy calms the mind, which doesn't need to go looking elsewhere for momentary happiness. I close my eyes in meditation again, and express gratitude for my senses—I can see, I can hear the hummingbird buzz up to the nearby feeder and give tiny satisfied chirps. Hearing a hummingbird "talk" is also thrilling. Then it zooms off.

Ten minutes later, I hear the telltale chirp and open my eyes to see the little guy sitting near me again. Awake to the day. Awake to joy.

STARS AND STAR FLOWERS

We tried three times to catch the Perseid meteor shower. On the night of the tenth, thin clouds wafted overhead; the night of the eleventh—the main night—was completely overcast; finally, on the twelfth, we lay out in the hammock for an hour, looking at the star-bejeweled sky. We saw only a couple of meteors, but my oh my, the fragrance of nicotiana nearby was intoxicating.

Flowering tobacco (*Nicotiana*) has simple star-shaped trumpet flowers that look rather plain-Jane all day. Then when the sun sets, they begin to pump out their perfume and fill the air with their sweet tropical scent.

The meteor shower was disappointing this year—weather conditions didn't permit us to see what we had hoped to see. Yet what could be lovelier than lying under the open sky star-gazing with my sweetie and inhaling the sweetness of nicotiana?

PLUMERIA/FRANGIPANI

I lived in Hawai'i for six months, many years ago, and I fell in love with plumeria, also called frangipani. When my parents visited, I made leis for them from the fragrant plumeria flowers.

Among my houseplants, I have plumeria, and it is blooming now. When a blossom falls off, I float it in a bowl of water until brown spots of aging appear. Then I compost it.

The tender, creamy white, fragrant flower arouses tender feelings in me. I still love that blossom even as it ages and withers.

When I lived in Hawai'i, I was a tender young thing with creamy skin, and I was in love. Now, my hands have brown age spots.

CHOCOLATE MINT REAPPEARS!

A friend gave me chocolate mint several years ago. I planted it at the edge of my mint patch, but then I lost it, since chocolate mint only grows to be about six inches tall and the neighboring, more vigorous, apple mint was four feet tall.

Now, after last summer's construction project, with two trenches dug through my former herb garden, chocolate mint has reappeared! It's growing about twelve feet away from its original location. One thing about mint: It's a survivor.

So, too, our sweet meditation practice can become lost in the overwhelming activity of daily life. Meditation is so small, and life is so big.

Yet, when disturbances strike—the eustress of good things or the distress of troublesome things—meditation survives to sustain and nourish us.

Allow meditation to reappear in your life today.

RIPPING OUT THE MINT

My non-gardening sweetie couldn't stand to look at the four-foot-tall mint patch that was falling over onto the kale, so he waded in and ripped out several armloads of mint. I carried it to the compost pile for him.

It's hard to watch stress overwhelm someone whom we care about. Perhaps we want to wade in and save her from her suffering. But, really, she has to pull the weeds out of her own (mental) garden. We can only offer our support in the process.

Stress is hard to live with, whether it's our own or the stress of someone we love. Our path is our own path. No one else can walk it for us.

Let's take a mindful walk in the garden and reduce our own stress.

photo credit: urf / iStock

LESSER AND GREATER HAPPINESS

This week began with three days of rain. Here in Vermont, evening temperatures have dropped from summer warm to polar-fleece cool. These conditions mean: Let the transplanting season begin (again)!

Now we have a couple of months (or more, if you're really hardy) to divide plants and move them around, thin out the overgrown colonies, and give the extras away or compost them.

The decision to divide clumps can be difficult. That mass of flowers looked so great when it was blooming in July. Now it's a mass of green leaves. In fact, it's mostly green background for five of the garden's six months. Other flowering plants need some space.

Sometimes we have to give up a lesser happiness in order to experience a greater happiness. In the garden, this can mean dividing a big clump of flowers. Yes, it brought us happiness for two or three weeks. But we might be happier if other flowers were blooming around it during the other five months of the gardening season.

In our lives, we give up the lesser happiness of "getting things done," Facebooking, or watching TV, in order to cultivate a secluded internal garden of meditative calm. This calm can carry over into our lives for minutes or hours as we build a new habit of greeting each day with joy.

HAVING FAITH

Last summer I bought a small hanging pot of portulaca. It was cute, but it didn't "hang" that well. The magenta flowers were in the pot, not hanging down the sides.

I over-wintered the flowerless succulent indoors. In the spring, I divided it and planted it as an edging, where it is now spectacular.

We undertake meditation hoping that it will bloom in our lives. At first, it may seem as though nothing is happening. But if we keep tending it, even during the dark and cold times, it will eventually flower and surprise us with the beauty of the calmed mind.

This is all the faith we need on this path. Neither faith in something unbelievable nor faith in something miraculous. Just the faith to sit and watch the present moment.

And then it blooms.

MEDITATING FROG

We went shopping for garden statues again, and this time my sweetie found a fun one. He's drawn to the naked young women and nymphs; I favor the Buddhas and sculptures honoring St. Francis and Mother Mary.

We found a meditating frog at the local farm and garden store. Perfect for the front step. Just the right combination of nature, spirit, and whimsy. I can't help but smile when I walk in the front door, and I hope visitors smile too.

"Breathing in, I calm body and mind.
Breathing out, I smile."

This verse reminds us to bring our attention back to the breath. Calming. Smiling. Whether we are sitting in meditation or walking in the front door.

RANDOM ACTS OF MINDFULNESS

My friend Ann has done a lot of traveling this summer—a week at the lake, a bike tour in Italy, a trip to Colorado. Now that she's home, she's having major repairs done to her house.

And her garden? "I do random acts of weeding," she says. "If I walk by a flowerbed and see a weed, I pull it. Then I just tuck it under a bush. Due to the construction, I've hardly been out in my backyard at all."

When life gets busy, sometimes all we have time for are random acts of gardening and random acts of mindfulness. As we walk by our flowerbeds, we are mindful of walking, of bending over, of pulling a weed.

When we are in the car, we can turn off the music or news, and, for five minutes, note our experience out loud. "Hearing." "Seeing." "Feeling." We hear the sounds of the external world. Distracted by a thought, we "hear" the internal world. Bringing ourselves back to the task at hand, we "see" the external world.

The mind wanders away. Visual thinkers may "see" the internal world as they are thinking or feeling or hearing. Once again, let's bring our attention to what we are doing: "Feeling" the hands on the steering wheel, "feeling" the sensations of sitting, "feeling" the tiny sensations of tension in the body as we drive in traffic.

Continue to label: Hearing. Seeing. Feeling.

In this way, we practice random acts of mindfulness and kindness.

NIGHTTIME NICOTIANA

The sensor floodlight flashes on when I pull into the driveway at night. I park my car under a hemlock tree and walk toward the front door and the white garden.

I didn't leave the front porch light on, so I'm guided by starlight and moonlight and the receding floodlight behind me.

The flowers of the white garden dance in the dark, and then I smell the heady fragrance of *Nicotiana*. "Ahhh," I say to the night sky.

During the day, *Nicotiana* isn't much of a flower to look at. It's a bit lanky, with single trumpet flowers seeming to cluster at the top, but then the stalk stretches up so there's a flower every inch or two. Since the leaves, stem, and flowers are sticky to the touch, I leave them alone.

When we close our eyes to meditate, it can seem a bit dark in there. And maybe it looks as if there's not much to "see." Perhaps our mind is a bit sticky. As we focus on the sensations in the body and the sounds around us, we may relax into calmness, if only for a few seconds. "Ahhh."

TEENAGE SQUASH

You can't leave the vegetable garden alone for one day. If you do, watch out! Those vegetables grow from babies to troublesome teenagers overnight. Then you have to deal with them—strictly and lovingly. Before we left for a long weekend, I grated ten big summer squashes. I came home four days later to find five more sizable squashes.

Firm, yet loving and accepting, parenting forecasts the best outcome for teens. Overdoing it in one way or the other spells trouble. How do we walk this fine line in our own daily lives?

We are not following an "If it feels good, do it" path or an "If it feels good, then it must be right" path. That's too much acceptance.

Nor are we forcing ourselves to meditate for 60 minutes at four o'clock in the morning, no matter what. That's too strict and makes the body (and mind) contract.

We practice kindness, yet we also have to make an effort. We aim for a consistency of practice: sitting about the same length of time (even if it's "only" five minutes) at about the same time every day.

Now I have to expend some more effort harvesting summer squash. Maybe I'll practice kindness, to myself, by giving them away.

RAINDROP MEDITATION

Yesterday I sat a daylong retreat with a meditation teacher I've been studying with for ten years. The gray morning soon yielded sprinkling rain—a relief for our parched gardens, and a sweet meditation object, too. Listening to raindrops brings me straight into the present moment. My mind feels refreshed.

My inner naturalist becomes interested in the habits and habitats of raindrops. Each raindrop I hear is actually the death of the raindrop as it becomes something else—a puddle, a wet streak on a window, damp earth. That raindrop has disappeared. It has passed away. Now it's a rivulet running downhill into a storm sewer, into a creek or river, and into the ocean.

As we exhale, the breath passes away, passes out of our bodies and joins the air surrounding us—air that is breathed by the person sitting next to us or transpired by the tree in the yard or the grass in the lawn.

Water. Air. It's me and mine for a moment. Then it's not. What happens to the me when it becomes the other?

HARVEST VS. VACATION

It happens every August and September: harvest season collides with vacation time.

Cherry tomatoes are dripping off the vine, and I leave home for two or three days to go to the lake or to the ocean. Green beans point their green fingers accusingly: *Are you leaving us on our own—again*? And do I dare leave the zucchini while I take a ten-day trip to the Grand Canyon?

The impermanence of fresh vegetables leads me straight to dukkha—wanting things to be other than they are. Wanting the vegetables to wait for me, wait until I'm ready for them. So, I e-mail my neighbors. "I'm abandoning my garden until Labor Day. Feel free to pick anything you want—tomatoes, chard, beans, squash, cabbage, beets, kale, peppers, cucumbers, and especially zucchini."

Generosity salves the sting of my garden's surplus.

SWEET ONIONS

This year my onions are all the size of baseballs. No weenie onions. Not one.

Of course, I expect the Walla Walla (Vidalia) onions to be that size, but the golden onions and the red onions are only marginally smaller—at least the size of tennis balls. Maybe this summer's heat relaxed all of them into rotundity. After all, the onion capitals of Walla Walla, Washington, and Vidalia, Georgia, are hot places. Whatever the cause, the conditions were excellent for onions this year.

Sometimes the conditions are just right for the skillful habits we want to grow in our own minds. Years may go by when the fruits of our meditation practice seem rather piddling. Then one sit or one stressful situation, perhaps one where we feel hot under the collar, and our new skillful habits save us. That's when we harvest the fruits of the spiritual life.

Did you know that some people eat those sweet Walla Walla onions (the onion-ring onion) like apples?

photo credit: rjlerich / iStock

WELCOME CUKES

The long cucumbers in the garden are long, all right: two feet long, and thick with seeds. Now: What to do with four of them?

This is the challenge of vegetable gardening. Either it *doesn't* grow—like my zucchini one year (can you believe it?) or it *does* grow abundantly—in which case, there's the dilemma of the over-supply. I figure it will take between one and two hours to work some magic on these cukes. They could become pickles. Salsa solves my tomato and pepper abundance.

The Garden Club is having a fund-raiser today at the Welcome Center on Interstate 91. Coffee and baked goods are welcome, surely, but travelers also love fresh fruit and fresh veggies in a plastic cup to go. Or hand them a sandwich baggie of tortilla chips to go with a cup of salsa and....

Welcome to our green state!

TOO MUCH

The tomato hornworms have returned to my garden. They're so well camouflaged that I haven't actually seen one yet, but I do see their handiwork—bare tomato stems.

The tomato hornworm eats tomato leaves. You have to admit that tomato leaves have a signature scent (and perhaps taste?) that draws us tomato-loving folk. On occasion, I've even bought tomato-leaf-scented soap.

The best way to control the tomato hornworm, I've found, is by planting a very limited section of flowering tobacco (*Nicotiana*) near the precious crop of tomatoes. This year, however, I let the nicotiana pop up everywhere it wanted to. Now I have too much of it.

The tobacco hornworm is very closely related to the tomato hornworm; my theory is that the flowering tobacco serves as an alternate host for the tomato hornworm.

But too much of anything leads to problems. Too much food (*I should diet.*), too many clothes (*What am I going to wear today?*), too much stuff around the house (*I can't find....*). Too many tomato hornworms.

It's time to prune the clutter. And it's time to pull out the flowering tobacco in and around the vegetable garden.

A MASTER GARDENER'S GARDEN

I love going to Master Gardener meetings—once I actually get myself there. The idea of trundling off to someone else's garden in the hills feels so out-of-the-way, so I've-got-other-things-to-do.

But I pull into the driveway and park beside five other cars. As I enter the 150-year-old farmhouse, I smell muffins baking. Our host, Steve, is describing the five tomato varieties he's growing this season. He's planted, among others, Moskvich, a Russian variety, because it's early, and Juliet, which is halfway between a grape tomato and an Italian tomato, because it's excellent for drying. He shows us his food dryer, which is about the size of a toaster oven.

Then we walk out to his vegetable garden, which is about 60 feet by 60 feet. In other words, bigger than his house. New Zealand spinach is difficult to germinate, he says, but it's volunteering in three beds other than where it was planted. I taste its tangy, thick leaf.

The eight people who have shown up ask intelligent questions, make astute observations, and share experiences. I am among people who know more about gardening than I do, and I am fascinated.

So, too, it's sometimes hard to drag ourselves to our meditation seat. The world is filled with "more important" things to do. Yet if we simply make the effort to do what we know is good for us, we put ourselves in a position to notice the joy of the inner garden and reap the fruits of mindfulness.

HURRICANE IRENE

Hurricane Irene has come and gone. It rained for 20 hours, beginning and ending with a couple of hours of mist.

I was kayaking on the Connecticut River looking for migrating nighthawks (none) before the rain started on Saturday evening. The water level at the confluence of the Connecticut and West Rivers was extremely low; the put-in place was a slender, shallow channel through mud flats.

During the last heavy rains, three years ago, all the boats and docks floated down to the dam, ten miles downriver. This time, it looked as though boat owners were playing it safe: all the boats, as well as the docks, had disappeared.

By noon on Sunday, rivers were flooding the banks, and stray docks were floating away one by one. Streams were also spilling over their banks and flooding the floodplains. Woe to people who had homes or businesses in low-lying areas.

The treetops waved wildly for about ten minutes, and I thought my eastern casement windows (closed but not locked) might rip off their hinges and fly away. The electricity went out, as we knew it would, but here for only three hours.

At noon, the rivers looked more solid than liquid, carrying away trees, branches, debris, and docks.

Our earth-ly bodies also float away, down the river of life. Two weeks ago, a writing friend learned she had liver cancer. She died a few days later.

A raindrop dies into a puddle, into a trickle, into a stream, the rivers into the floodplain. We, too, die; the ego dies into the ocean of impersonal space that surrounds us.

PEACH FANTASY

Twenty years ago, a gardening friend gave me a little peach tree, which I squeezed into a not very sunny spot at the back of a flowerbed. I eagerly awaited my first peaches, but the raccoons got to them first.

A few years later, a branch, laden with young fruit, split off. (This branch-breaking is common with peach trees. The trees in the nearby peach orchard lose heavy branches every year.) But this year our tree lost its one remaining branch, which broke off, heavily laden with small green peaches.

How many things do we squeeze into our lives, seeking to savor the sweetness of material goods, friends, travel, luscious peaches?

Yet, things don't always yield as we had hoped.

It's time to cut down the peach tree. It's time to renounce my fantasy of home-grown peaches.

What, in your daily life, is it time to renounce?

photo credit: nata_zhekova / iStock

NASTURTIUM SEEDS

It's time to gather nasturtium seeds. This year I planted a variety I particularly like: Butter Cream, which is a pale yellow. If I delay until September, I won't be able to find the seeds. Now is the time.

The wrinkled, roundish, green seeds grow two or three to a stem, but several have already dropped onto the ground. If you live where winters are mild (such as in the Pacific Northwest), your nasturtiums will reseed themselves. Here in Vermont, where winters can be severe, nasturtium seeds must be planted intentionally.

Nasturtiums are high in vitamin C, so if I feel a sniffle, I go directly to the nasturtiums and munch the peppery leaves as well as the flowers.

The seeds of mindfulness that we plant every day also have the power to protect us from the ills of life, beginning with protection from ill-will. Your mother told you to count to ten; mindfulness encourages us to simply notice how irritation, frustration, and anger feel in the body.

Yes, the symptoms of ill feeling still arise, but instead of exploding or imploding, we take the middle way. Dare to "feel" how irritation touches the body: Unpleasant, yes. And what else? Where is the tightness, the tension, located? Mindfulness encourages us to look with interest instead of reactivity. If nothing else, simply note your experience: "Irritation. Irritation. Irritation." Or "Frustration. Frustration." And even: "Anger. Anger."

Notice that the ill feeling arises. (Well, that's the easy part.) Notice that it ceases. Then it's gone. Maybe it's only gone for a moment, or maybe it's gone for good.

Mindfulness is the vitamin that protects us from dis-ease.

LISTEN TO THE SOUND OF THE FALLING RAIN

This morning it's raining.

Let's listen to the rain as it falls. This is a wonderful listening meditation. Close your eyes and soak into the sound of rain raining.

Notice the "flow" of sound that comes and goes so fast it's nearly impossible to separate out individual sounds.

First: zoom out to the panoramic sound of the rain falling. Then, try zooming in to the raindrop level. Every time you lose the close-up focus, zoom out to the more panoramic sound.

Contemplate the life cycle of a single raindrop, beginning with what you can see. A raindrop comes into view. It plops onto a window or the ground and loses its raindrop-ness. Gone. That raindrop is gone; it just died into a puddle, into a trickle, into a stream.

Notice gone-ness. Gone. Gone. Gone.

THE STORMS OF LIFE

Jim's deep backyard ends at a stream that makes a right-angle turn. You could say that his backyard is bounded by a burbling brook on two sides.

That sedate creek became a raging river during Hurricane Irene. When Jim left for church, the brook was turbulent; when he returned, a flash flood was raging: water covered his football-field-sized backyard and was racing into his garage. He was able to close the back door of the garage, holding off a wall of water that was pouring in. Then he watched as a fifteen-foot-long brush pile he'd been accumulating floated off, turning slightly into the back of his garage, effectively forming a barrier that looked like a beaver dam, now held in place by the force of the water.

In our meditation practice, we eventually learn to recognize the debris of our thoughts floating down the river of consciousness. Sometimes, when we are flooded by the waters of emotion, our mindfulness is strong enough to protect us. We decide we can tolerate the turbulent emotion for one minute, or two, or even ten minutes, and so we manage to watch the flood.

An emotion has two parts—body sensations (often unpleasant) and a thought (very slippery). We decide to observe just one of these.

We watch body sensations—we notice the tension, the tightness; or we watch the bumpy, smooth, rough, short, or shallow breath.

If our mindfulness is strong, we watch thoughts go by, like downed trees in a swollen river. That thought, which seemed so strong and sturdy and true, actually comes into view, floats by us rapidly, and disappears. Gone.

The next thought rushes by, again gathering all our attention and even our belief in it; then it, too, disappears.

Mindfulness is our ally during the storms of life.

GRAPE TOMATOES

I've come to a deeper appreciation of grape tomatoes this week. I grow them specifically to sun-dry them. I like their firm meatiness. As I halved hundreds of cherry tomatoes for the food dryer, I noticed that, for the most part, the grape tomatoes were stemless, while about half the Sun Golds still had their attachments—their stems.

What is it about our attachments? Sometimes we can detach from the mother ship (or mother plant) or any situation in our lives, and go on to the next moment.

But sometimes we are still carrying our attachment to what was said in yesterday's meeting or what was done (or undone) last week. We cling to these sorts of attachments and can't shake them off, even though we know it would be a whole lot better for our mental health if we could just "let go."

Let's focus on letting go of the guilt or the opinions we keep raking over, or the hurt that is creating sorrow or distress for us.

If the grape tomato can just let go, can we?

SURPRISE!

I like surprises, so back in May I bought a pack of "Heirloom" tomatoes at the Farmers' Market. Which heirlooms? Only time would tell.

I couldn't quite believe my eyes when I saw the first yellow tomato in the vegetable garden. Yellow? What's a yellow tomato doing in *my* garden? Oh, right. The heirlooms!

My dad loved yellow tomatoes, but I would never willingly eat one. I have to say, though, that yellow tomatoes are surprisingly tasty. Another plant bears yellow tomatoes with green stripes. Then there's the coral-colored tomato that's green on top. I keep waiting for it to ripen, but it only rots. Oh! It's supposed to be coral and green, so I eat it green.

Our lives are full of surprises, although we like to think we are in control. With all the choices available to us nowadays, we think we should get what we want. Certainly *not* yellow tomatoes!

But no one can predict the future. This bothers our minds tremendously: we feel anxious, worried, restless, and fearful when we consider the future. I don't even know—for sure—what I'm going to eat for breakfast in 20 minutes.

Stay in the present moment. It's the only place we can ever be, anyway. Let the now surprise you.

PEPPERS LIKE IT HOT

Returning from a hot vacation in the Southwest, I go out to the vegetable garden, and find a dozen red peppers, plus another dozen somewhere on the green-yellow-red spectrum. In a Vermont garden, such as mine, I treasure red peppers. With our short growing season, green peppers are a cinch, but waiting for peppers to turn orange, yellow, purple, or red can be chancy, because peppers like it hot. Fortunately, this summer has been hot.

Given the proper conditions, our meditation practice will also ripen in time, and we can harvest the fruits (or vegetables) of a spiritual life. The question is: How long is our growing season?

Let's allow our meditation to ripen now, in the summer of our lives.

photo credit: Jtasphoto / iStock

WHEN DOES YOUR MEDITATION PRACTICE BLOOM?

Over the years, I've tried a wide variety of annuals—for color, but I find I return to those few that bloom predictably for me: begonias in the sandy soil beside the basement door, and impatiens in the semi-shade of the north side of the house.

In my cutting beds, I rely on certain annuals to volunteer year after year—poppies, bachelor buttons, spider flower (*Cleome*), nicotiana, love-in-a-mist (*Nigella*). In recent years, I have planted zinnias for their reliability and range of color.

I have given up on some of annuals I love: Cosmos bouquets disappoint me because they are so short-lived. For years, I thought geraniums and portulaca should bloom in a hot, dry spot; but they don't. I now put my geraniums in a pot on the front stoop, and think the Swiss are onto something with their red geraniums in white window boxes.

When we are learning to meditate, we may try various teachers and approaches to meditation. Over time, we find that one school of meditation fits us better than another, even though our friends have gone on to something else. We let go of the approaches to spiritual practice that don't quite bloom for us, even though they do for other people.

We feel more at home with particular teachings. We settle into our choice. And our own practice flowers.

HARVESTING. OR NOT.

In May, a vendor at the local Farmers' Market offered five different varieties of basil seedlings for $2 per paper cup filled with a dozen tiny plants. So I bought all five types. (Desire.)

Regular basil
Purple basil
Lemon basil
Thai basil
Sacred basil (a.k.a. Tulsi)

Just imagine the delicious pesto, fish, or Thai curry I could cook! (Delusion)

But with so many other plants to care for, by the time I turned my attention to the basil, it was late August and the basil was flowering. (Aversion, because you're supposed to pick basil *before* it flowers.)

Yesterday I harvested the lemon basil, put it through the food processor, and froze it in little containers. (Happiness.)

This morning I harvested the purple basil. But does anyone really want to eat purple pasta? (Doubt.)

Today I'm turning my attention to sacred basil, which has a very slight anise undercurrent to the main basil flavor. Hmmm. Licorice pasta? (Doubt *and* aversion.) In the Ayurvedic system, sacred basil (tulsi) is used to make teas and tinctures. (Desire for a good idea.)

Harvesting continues in fits and starts. Doubt, aversion, and worry slow me down. Sense desire (pesto!) speeds me up.

When you bring mindfulness to the harvest of **your** garden, what do you find? What vegetables or flowers languish? Which vegetables or flowers actually get picked? Once they are picked, what happens?

The five hindrances of desire, aversion, laziness, worry, and doubt slow us down—on the cushion or in the garden.

BASIL PESTO

I'm making pesto, one half pint at a time. I go out to the garden, harvest a few branches of basil, bring them into the kitchen, and grind them up with olive oil in the food processor.

In the past, I have overloaded myself by picking too much basil at once, then become distracted, eventually returning to a basketful of wilted leaves.

The small-steps method means more steps out to the garden and back, but, for me, it's more strategic than the extravaganza method of harvesting three or four basil bushes and then becoming overwhelmed.

Mindfulness leads us to small steps of insight and gradually awakens us, so that we can let go of one stressor and then another.

I'm letting go of the idea that I *must* harvest all my basil before the frost. One branch at a time, one half pint at a time. So far, I've frozen a gallon of pesto.

THAI FOOD

When I go to the Farmers' Market, I always stop at the Thai food booth to buy red curry to eat and a fish custard as take-away.

Now I'm harvesting Thai basil and freezing it as pesto, so I can make my own Thai food.

Meditation is a do-it-yourself exercise. You can't go out and buy a calm mind, no matter how many times you go to hear the Dalai Lama (or any other spiritual teacher).

I love Thai food, and I love the Dalai Lama. Now if I can just love meditation enough to sit myself down every day, I'll soon be harvesting the flavor of a spiritual life.

photo credit: thatreec / iStock

FAREWELL TO HUMMINGBIRDS

The hummingbirds have left. Like summer people, they live here in the North Country from May 10 to September 10—only four months of the year. Yet I am so happy to see them come, and so sad to see them go.

I was walking through my herb garden on September 8, when a hummingbird flew toward me, hovered in front of my face for five seconds, then zoomed off.

Wow! I thought, and *Odd.*

A few days later, I realized that I hadn't seen a hummingbird since. She must have been saying, "Farewell, and thanks for all the flowers. See you next year. We're leaving now. Bye."

DRY GARDENS; DRY MEDITATION

Ordinarily I would have begun transplanting perennials and shrubs three weeks ago. I would have been dividing bunches of phlox and mums, and merrily moving short or tall plants to their proper class-photo place in a flowerbed. But we are still faced with a drought here in New England.

In our neighborhood, a backhoe digging down four feet found only dryness. Dug wells, ten or twelve feet deep, have dried up as the water table has sunk, and the people in those homes are having to buy water. Quite an unusual event for this normally green Green Mountain State where I live.

My sweetie beseeches me to water the gardens—a daunting task that makes me wish I had set up an irrigation system.

Sometimes our meditation practice feels dry. This is when we're tempted to give up meditating. Maybe we'll decide to try something juicier—psychic readings, enneagrams, astrology, jogging.

How do we water a dry practice? Consider finding a new object of meditation or changing your meditation posture.

Make walking or standing meditation your main form. Or if you are daring, try lying-down meditation; or do a body scan.

Change your object of meditation to hearing or to sensations. Or spend a year practicing loving-kindness. If you experience a dry spell, move to compassion. If that dries up, practice appreciative joy. Then equanimity. And start again.

Commit to a teacher, and call or e-mail her once a month. If you can, sign up for a retreat, if only for a weekend, a day, or part of a day.

My mind is such that I find investigation very interesting. Take a high-lighted or underlined phrase from the spiritual book you are reading, and spend your entire meditation session contemplating that. Go ahead and turn it over in your mind, word by word, phrase by phrase.

Water your practice now. Trust me. You will see blooms by next summer.

MONEY PLANT MAGIC

Money plant (*Lunaria*) has gone to seed, its flat oblong brown pods clinging to stiff stems. I go out now to my flowerbed and uproot this dead biennial until I have a handful of stalks. Then I shake them over the flowerbed like a magic wand. *Abracadabra. Next year I want flowers* here!

The seed membranes fly off and float to earth. A few shakes later, all that remains in my hand is a bouquet of silver "coins" on a stem, luminescent in the sunny, cool late-summer day. Without spending any money on flower seeds or on seedlings, my garden will have blooms aplenty next spring.

THE SWEETNESS OF SUN-DRIED TOMATOES

I have an extravaganza of cherry tomatoes, so I cut them in half to "sun-dry" them in my food dryer. In fact, I grow the meaty grape cherry tomatoes expressly for drying, rather than eating fresh. These sun-dried tomato chips are packed with enough flavor to make your taste buds stand up and say, "Hooray!"

As we condense our meditation into concentration, the essential "flavor" of attention is experienced as sweetness.

I store the sun-dried tomatoes in plastic bags in the refrigerator, so that on some cold winter's evening I can taste the sweet flavor burst of summer's tomatoes.

photo credit: anamaria63 / iStock

DIRT IN THE TRUNK

Now is the time to make a last trip to the garden center to buy those perennials or shrubs that can hardly wait to shrug off their containers like outgrown coats.

Great deals are there for the spending, under the disguise of "**Save 50%.**" We could save 100 percent by not buying anything, but desire trumps logic any day.

So we load plants into the trunk of our car, maybe overflowing onto the floor of the back seat. Some women carry the protection of an old shower curtain or an old rug, but I always was an au-naturel girl. After I arrive home and unload, crumbs of dirt and a dead leaf or two remind me day after day, week after week, to clean up after myself.

Desire is the culprit that weakens our integrity, that pushes us to tell a white lie, to fudge a bit, to keep the incorrect change that is given, to kill pests because we hate them, to drink one glass of wine too many.

Our conscience knows. Our conscience has the integrity to notice our crummy behavior. But we throw those thoughts into the trunk of our mind and try not to notice.

When we finally get around to cleaning up our act, we feel so much better. Ahhh! We can breathe again.

GIVING AWAY ZUCCHINIS

Zucchinis are a joke in my community. Once I found a big green dude strapped into my passenger seat with a seat belt. After a carpenter friend had fixed some lighting in the bedroom, I found a baseball bat of a zucchini under my pillow. I myself have left zucchinis anonymously in neighbors' mailboxes.

You might call this generosity. Or you might not.

There are three types of generosity: "cheapo" giving, which says, "I'm going to get rid of this anyway, so I might as well give it to you." Then there's the medium level of giving, which is sharing something that is valuable to you with others. However, regal giving, or *raja dana*, is the most powerful form of giving. It is giving what is most precious to you.

While putting surplus zucchinis in unexpected places is good for a laugh, my heart feels happy when I give my extra vegetables to the local food bank. And I feel very happy when I share the dharma teachings that are most precious to me.

ROOTS OF STRESS
AT THE END OF THE SEASON

Thirty-six hours ago, the temperature here was 88 degrees, and I was in the neighbors' swimming pool. This morning, frost is predicted in low-lying areas.

The good thing about predictions is that they light a fire under my intentions. Yesterday, in the rain, I picked all my peppers and harvested two basil bushes.

Temperatures have dropped suddenly and sharply, meaning I have to harvest what's left of my hot-weather crops—or risk losing them. I cannot loll around hoping for an endless summer. The cucumber vines have died. So have the tomato plants. I pulled out all the pepper plants (still green) yesterday. Basil is next. I cut zinnia bouquets every day.

I could take the route of aversion, and just give up on the gardens. *Forget it! Too much work!*

I could take the route of greediness and think, "I'm going to harvest every single thing, turn my kitchen into a food preparation workshop, and fill my freezer to overflowing."

Or I could take the route of delusion and not even notice the weather.

Delusion. Aversion. Greed. These are the roots of stress in daily life.

I nod to each one as it shows up in my life and in my garden.

"Oh, hello, Delusion. You think I should wait a few more days just in case hot weather returns?"

"Hello, my good old friend Aversion. You think I should just give up and call it quits? You're too tired to do anything?"

"Oh, my dear friend Greed. So good to see you again. I see you have lots of plans that entail me harvesting everything, preparing it beautifully, and cooking delicious meals."

Mindfulness recognizes each one, and smiles.

SUN AND SHADE

In the summer, I go out to the garden in the early morning. By 10:00, the heat of the sun drives me into the shade.

Now, in the autumn, I stay indoors until the sun rises above the trees surrounding my house. I go out to the garden in the middle of the day. When the long shadows of nearby trees begin to cover the lawn, I seek out the last sunny spots and do my gardening there.

Sometimes working in the sun is pleasant; sometimes, unpleasant.

Sometimes shade is pleasant; sometimes, unpleasant.

Pleasant and unpleasant rule our actions. This gut response decides for us, and then the mind (a.k.a. the ego) takes ownership and tries to define itself: "I'm a sun worshiper." or "I try to stay out of the sun." But really, we are not one or the other. Most often, we are both…and…

I am loving these warm autumn days with a cool breeze blowing.

Pleasant.

WHICH PATH?

My partner Bill and I go outdoors together, and engage in parallel play and work. He does wood; I do dirt. He looks up to the trees around our house; I look down to flowers and weeds.

Occasionally we call to each other, "Hey! I need a consultation over here." We enjoy the benefit of an extra set of eyes, another mind with creative ideas.

In the evening, after dinner, we stroll through the garden. He plans which branches to prune; I decide which plants I want to move. The effect is gracious, as he subtracts trees at the edge of the woods, while I add flowering plants.

Our friends may follow a different spiritual path than we do, yet we still may gain from the cross-fertilization of meditation and contemplation. Although I am completely happy with my path of Theravadin Buddhism (from Southeast Asia), and I highly recommend it, I never cease to be amazed at the different doors that people walk through. One friend loves Thich Nhat Hanh. Another feels "Tibetan;" so that path obviously fits him better. And then there's that out-of-the-box Zen friend.

Never mind that our minds don't work in the same ways. We can call on our spiritual friends for consultation in our lives when we need that. Our mutual goal is kindness.

SHROUDED IN MIST

I live on the high shoulder of a river valley; at this time of year, morning dawns gray to reveal rising mist. The body of earth and, specifically, the nearby body of water are slowly losing their heat into the air.

Red and yellowed leaves are falling on my flowerbeds as if to season them with a dash of colored pepper. At the same time, heat is rising from earth and from water in the form of vapor.

Earth, water, air, and heat (also called fire). I watch the interplay of these four "elements," which are actually the three forms of matter—solid, liquid, and gas—plus the heat required to transubstantiate one element into another.

River water transmutes into water vapor, losing its heat in the process—the death of summer. It's a slower process than the death of the physical body. One of the signs of impending death is that our body loses its heat. "People die from the feet up," my father told me. The body first withdraws heat from its extremities.

Steam rises from the teacup in my hand as I gaze out the window at the backyard, shrouded in mist.

HARVEST BEFORE FROST

The race is on to see how much I can harvest before the frost. This morning's temperature was 40 degrees.

Really, there's not much left in the garden, and that's good, because there's not much space left in the freezer.

The tomatoes are in, leaving just a basketful of cherry tomatoes on the vine. The winter squashes are in, but one gourd vine went crazy. I try to bring in one gourd every time I return from the garden. Then there are my eight varieties of basil.

We plant many seeds during our lifetime—friends, family, career, spiritual path, service to others. Which shall we harvest? And which do we just let go of?

Many friends come and go. Our career ends. Family changes its definition: our parents die, our siblings drift into the distance, wives and husbands divorce, our children grow up, our grandchildren live far away. Who *is* our true family?

Our spiritual path may ebb and flow, yet it gives us the ability to harvest kindness, mindfulness, and equanimity, no matter the season.

FALL

WELCOME FALL!

Welcome to Fall! Here in Vermont, leaves are tinged with yellow, orange, and red, hinting at the glorious colors to come.

When we first begin to meditate, we may receive just a taste of relaxation or joy. Then the mind gets busy and that luscious taste fades. *Oh, I can't do it right*, we may think.

But when we take the time to pause in our lives—and perhaps sit with our eyes closed for just five minutes—we are developing the muscle of mindfulness that enables us to fall into calmness or happiness with grace.

photo credit: fotojog / iStock

FIRST DAY OF FALL

Today is the first full day of fall. To celebrate, I picked up eight pots of chrysanthemums on my way home from the airport. The houseplants have come indoors. The mums now sit on the front step. It's official. A new season has arrived.

Sometimes, the seasons of our lives have official markers—birthdays, anniversaries, graduations, marriages. We remember the day when a child was born or a parent died, but often, it seems, we recall little noticeable difference between one day and another.

"Noticing" is another word for mindfulness. We notice not only the big changes—of season, of leaving home and arriving at work—we also notice the small, incremental changes. The light in the room is changing. Right now. The breath in your body is changing. Right now. Your heart is beating. Right now. Your eyes are shifting their focus. Right now.

I'm going outdoors now to notice the changes in the gardens. The tomato vines have died. The production of summer squash has slowed. The broccoli and chard look ecstatic, now that the weather has cooled a few degrees.

Simply sit still for a minute, and notice life. Your life—and the life around you.

CHANGE OF PLANTS

The houseplants came indoors yesterday, after a good long summer vacation of more than four months. The Dieffenbachia looks great. The banana tree is nearly six feet tall.

I had to make some hard decisions: There's just not enough room in my jam-packed solarium for a four-foot-tall jade plant. I'm sending it off to the local garden club's plant sale on Saturday. But first, I sawed off a side shoot, which was 18 inches tall; I'm keeping that little(r) plant. The bird-of-paradise, which blooms when it is pot-bound, busted out of its container this summer. I divided it into four pots, one of which I'll keep.

Change. Change of season. Change of plants. Change of plans—the re-potting took longer than expected.

All around us, life is in constant flux. Although we may not notice it, we, too, are constantly changing. Since arising this morning, you've probably changed your clothes or changed your mind about something (maybe about the clothes you were wearing). Breath has changed; blood has changed; bodily fluids have changed—some of been eliminated, some have been added. I'm drinking tea as I write this.

Summer vacation is truly over. Some day, the summer of our lives will drift away.

Welcome fall.

HARVEST: BOUNTY OR COMPOST?

In this harvest season, I try to cook two or three vegetables from the garden for dinner every evening—broccoli or zucchini, chard or kale, and a salad entirely of tomatoes. I leave the leftovers in the fridge for my sweetie. When I return from a long weekend away, they're still there.

"You're supposed to have eaten these," I say, with one eye on the overflowing harvest basket I just brought in from the vegetable garden.

"Oh, I did," he says. "Except for that yellow squash. You deal with that."

This is when our delight in the garden's bounty takes a dive into exasperation. Too much of a good thing leads to some form of suffering or another. I spend an hour after dinner slicing tomatoes for the food drier or blanching broccoli for the freezer.

Speaking of which, we've just purchased a new seven-cubic-foot Energy Star freezer because we had so much too much food to freeze.

FINAL GARDEN TOUR OF THE SEASON

Perennial Swappers, a local garden group, toured my fall garden this evening. "You're the bookends of the season," someone said gaily.

Swappers visit my spring garden on the first Thursday in May, when every gardener's green fingers are itching. And they visit again on the Thursday after the fall equinox. In our little community, the garden-touring season begins and ends in my garden.

"Aren't you bored with my gardens?" I asked the organizer. "Wouldn't you like to visit someone else's garden?"

But while most green thumbs are bemoaning a lack of color, I still have plenty. Blue monkshood towers over pink turtlehead, which mixes with magenta phlox and is framed by tall blue-purple asters. Violet ironweed blooms nearby.

White chenille stalks of *Sanguisorba* point skyward like candles crowded on a birthday cake. Pale pink *Anemone robustissima* floats above it all.

In the yellow garden, cup plant (*Silphium*) has nearly ended its reign as the tallest flower in the garden, while a colony of nearby helenium are winning the beauty contest with their crimson coronas. Redbud's heart-shaped leaves are already yellowing.

While many gardeners are now throwing in the trowel, I'm readying my garden for two more months of serious dividing and transplanting.

CHILI VERMONT

Tomatillos. I suppose they really should be grown south of the border, at least south of Vermont, where I live. But these green tomatoes in a husk reseed themselves prolifically in my vegetable garden. I let them have their way because I love chili verde. The green sauce and green salsa that you find in Mexican restaurants are made with tomatillos.

In August and September I dice them into homemade salsa. Now I'm cleaning up the vegetable garden in preparation for the first frost, and harvesting hundreds of these tomatillos still in their green husks. I store them in my unheated basement, and they will last until this time next year. No canning. No freezing. All I have to do is remember that I have fresh vegetables downstairs, waiting to jump into the chili pot, roll into goulash, or spike into Spanish rice. In the winter, I use tomatillos in any dish I would normally cook with tomatoes.

So when I go back to the garden, to that profusion of tomatillo vines, and I frown, "Ai-yi-yi! What was I thinking when I didn't weed these out in June?" I just have to change the accent. "Ai-yi-yi-yi. Canta, no llores." I'll sing for my supper—Chili Verde-mont tonight.

ZINNIAS—CUT AND COME AGAIN

"Oh, your zinnias are so beautiful," my friend Fair says.

Somehow, this year, I wound up with both dwarf and giant, single and double, quilled and pom-pom. Zinnias are quite a rewarding cut flower—a colorful vase-full lasts for a week. One variety is called "Cut and Come Again."

What's rewarding about our meditation practice? The calm. The decrease in anxiety and irritability. The solitude. The "centering."

Every day, let's cut out of the busy world for just a few minutes and come again to that quiet (and sometimes *not* so quiet!) place that nourishes us.

Zinnias rest the eyes. Meditation rests the body.

photo credit: Heather Powers / iStock

GREEN MULCH

As usual, the vegetable garden was out of control for several months this summer. It now looks more like a jungle than a picture postcard. So, well-armed with intention, I wade into the waist-high greenery and start pulling.

The culprits are not so much weeds, although there are some that escaped my attention and are now going to seed. Tomatillos sprawl everywhere. In our short northern season, only a few fruits on each plant are big enough to harvest. I pull out the plants wholesale, and pile them up in the middle of the garden. Self-seeding arugula has also gone wild, and I tug one plant out every three or four feet.

I pile all this greenery in the tomato bed and voila! Green mulch.

Sitting down to meditate can also feel like wading waist-deep through a thicket. Our mindfulness mulch consists of noticing each thought—not as a distraction to our breath meditation, but as another opportunity for mindfulness. "There you are, Irritation." "I see you, Worry." "There, there, Anxiety." Simply call these hindrances by name.

Proceeding step by step, through the garden or through our meditation, we clear a space and take a deep breath. Ahhh.

STORING LIFE AWAY

We had our first fire in the wood stove a couple of mornings ago, just to take the chill off. Even though it's not really cold yet, it's time for long sleeves and long pants. I'm storing summer clothes away bit by bit—shorts, short-sleeved shirts, tank tops, Capri pants.

Out in the vegetable garden, I'm trying to store summer away. Last night, I made lemon basil pesto and stored it in the freezer.

We try to store our lives away—in memories and in photo albums, on flash drives and on Facebook. These give us the illusion of a continuum. We think we can just reach back and touch our past. Yet our lives unfold moment by moment. The past is gone, never to be touched again.

Now there is only this person, with a memory that is evolving in the present moment.

FOUR-SEASON GARDENING

I was part of a community garden this summer, but before we even started, a local farmer came to talk to the six of us. "There's the spring garden, the summer garden, and the fall garden," he said.

We were particularly glad to hear about the summer garden, since we had already missed the spring garden by a wide swath. It was July 1st when the first person planted the first seed. Well, she'd been nurturing squash plants, cucumber vines, and tomatoes in pots on her patio. She was really happy to put those babies in the ground. And I was really happy that she planted her extra butternut squash seedlings in my 9'x12' plot.

In my vegetable garden at home, I'm just now clearing away the summer vegetables in anticipation of the first frost. Suddenly, I see the fall garden that's been hiding underneath and behind all that green and browning camouflage: rainbow chard, carrots, beets, broccoli, and kale. One pumpkin vine has run amok, twisting around the garden like intestines, and I have the best pumpkin crop I've ever had. Gourd vines have wound themselves over the back fence, so I have a good supply of seasonal decorations.

Spring, summer, fall. There is even a winter garden. Two years ago, my seven-year-old granddaughter wanted to go dig something out of the garden for dinner on the day after Christmas. There we were at 5:00, flashlights in mittened hands, digging up leeks and parsnips. A voice called to us through the dim evening, and my gardening neighbor, Connie, snowshoed up to see what we were doing. Gardening in the snow, of course.

PEAK FOLIAGE

Peak foliage season has arrived. After two years of so-so colors, this fall the foliage is spectacular. The red and yellow leaves against a blue sky are gorgeous!

People travel from afar just to experience the autumn color. In the past two days, I've met tourists from California, Louisiana, and Switzerland.

We expend a lot of energy to travel. We see the sights, and then we're gone. We are left with a memory that fades with time, a few photos that we don't look at again for quite a while, and a few feelings of happiness, fun, or relaxation.

And then, they disappear—the seeing, the hearing, the feeling—along with the colorful leaves that rain down to the ground in the next gust of wind.

We are searching for something, and we call it "travel." Perhaps we will find "it" there. Or there.

And all the time, right here, the "it" for which we are searching is traveling beside us and within us—a peaceful, joy-filled awareness.

THE FALL GARDEN

Broccoli is blooming in the vegetable garden. Now that the summer garden (tomatoes, cucumbers, beans, and summer squash) has been pulled out, I can see the fall garden—broccoli, kale, carrots, Brussels sprouts, and chard.

When we retire from the summer of our busy lives, we can see the fruits of our labors more clearly. We can enjoy the harvest: spending time with grandchildren, at volunteer jobs, or on our spiritual practice. Now we have time for the activities that gladden our hearts.

Let's eat lots of cancer-preventing broccoli and cholesterol-lowering kale. The fall garden is so much more relaxing than the summer garden.

photo credit: ouchi_iro / iStock

THE STINK OF LIFE

While slicing and dicing vegetables for salsa, which I call Garden in a Bowl, I encountered a few rotten tomatoes, rotten onions, and rotten peppers. The rot was just beginning, so I cut off the smelly, brown parts and salvaged the rest.

It's amazing, isn't it? Out of that smelly rot springs new life. Green onion tops were growing out of stinky brown, gushy onion layers.

Yet, all too often we try to eradicate what is smelly. I grew up taking one or two baths a week, with Mom washing my hair once a week. Nowadays, everyone showers every day, and we forget the smelliness of life unless we're alone in the bathroom with our bodies. We seem to believe that cleanliness is the natural state, and feel quite uncomfortable with our sweat and other natural by-products of the body.

But what is living smells (bad breath, farts, post-sex juices, underarms, crotches, feet). Before we erase this lesson from consciousness with the ease of a shower and some fragrant shampoo, let's inhale life in all its richness, both stinky and sweet.

Inhale now.

What do you smell?

BUTTERNUT STRESS AND BUTTERNUT CALM

Harvesting winter squash and pumpkins is like looking for hidden Easter eggs. The long vines winding off into the tall grass that had grown up around them meant that initially I missed a few butternut squashes. After my sweetie mowed that tall grass, I found a perfectly good squash that had been sheared right in half by the lawn mower. So, we had Butternut Black Bean Burritos for dinner. Delicious!

Our meditation practice can get lost in the tall grass of our busy lives. Then unexpected stresses come along, and there's nothing left for us to do but meditate. Today. Now.

Taste just a moment of delicious calm that reminds us that, yes, we are indeed sane. Behind the chatter or meanness of our "monkey minds" lies one second of peace. That tiny second is our vacation from "The Mind," which seeks to overwhelm us with its opinions and beliefs, over and over and over. In that jungle mind, there is a still forest pool. Under that tidal wave of beliefs, the ocean is calm. And so are we.

THE SCARF OF MANY COLORS

Margot gave me a pot of pink mums! What a delightful act of generosity.

I see 84-year-old Margot every week when our writing group meets, and we often compliment each other on our clothes or earrings, because we love the same bright reds, greens, and blues. Last November, I was wearing a multicolored scarf that coordinated well with my personal Joseph's-coat-of-many-colors, and Margot exclaimed, "I love your scarf!" I took it off and draped it around her neck. When she protested, I said, "You wear it this winter. I'll wear it next winter."

At this week's writing group, Margot returned the scarf to me for the season. She also gave me the pot of pink mums, for which I had just been silently wishing. Pretty soon, she and I won't even remember to whom the scarf "really" belongs.

GRATEFUL GENEROSITY

Several years ago, I bought variegated forsythia. I didn't have a place to plant it, so I stashed it in my nursery bed. And there it stayed. One little shrub-let became four good-sized bushes. You know how forsythia multiplies: a long branch touches the ground and roots. Pretty soon you have a forest of forsythia.

I transplanted two of them. Then I put the word out to sister gardeners: Come and get them. Today, the last one departs for another home and garden.

Giving away forsythia may sound like generosity, but I feel the recipients are doing me as big a favor as I am doing them. They're cleaning out a corner of my nursery bed, and for that I am very grateful.

IN THE SPOTLIGHT AND IN THE SHADOW

The houseplants are all indoors, including the flowerpots from the front step. My solarium looks like a jungle. I love the lushness.

"Too many," says my sweetie. He prefers that each plant stand alone, so that it can be seen in its fullness. This is the "specimen" approach to gardening.

I prefer the cottage garden approach—many plants in a small space. When something blooms, I bring it front and center, into the spotlight. Until then, it stands in the wings, awaiting its turn. And yes, some of my plants are professional wallflowers; they always stand against the wall.

Sometimes we are called upon to stand in the spotlight. Sometimes we are called upon to be a supporter in the shadows. One is not better than the other. How can we walk the middle path?

At the end of your meditation, take a few minutes to contemplate the following loving-kindness phrases:

> "humble and not conceited,
> contented and easily satisfied…
> not proud and demanding in nature…."

How does each apply to your life?

My houseplants are standing, some at the back, some at the front. They have no preferences.

DELICIOUS KIWIS

The frost has yet to come. I'm still buying local kiwi fruits at the farm stand. Since kiwis are a relatively new crop locally, our farm stand markets them as "kiwi berries" and has a sample basket next to the cash register. "Try one."

Still, people hesitate to try them. My sweetie, Bill, encourages a mother to sample one, but she gives it to her ten-year-old son. "Interesting," he says. Then Bill offers another one to the mom. "Mmmm," she says, and he gently places a little tub of kiwis in her shopping basket. (He's a born salesman, that Bill.)

We hesitate when we encounter a new path. We doubt it. We're afraid of something—distaste, harm, or "wrong-ness."

That's the reason why we venture onto the path of meditation one step at a time. First, we sit down, close our eyes, and watch our breath for a few minutes. Our mind has other ideas. Lots of them. So, perhaps we consult a book, a YouTube video, a teacher, and find we are in exactly the right place.

As we build confidence, in kiwi berries or in meditation, we walk farther and farther down the path. Eventually, we might even admit: it's delicious, that calm.

FROST TONIGHT

The forecast of frost tonight puts me in high gear: I need to pick the last of the basil and the tomatillos and anything else that's tender—today. And the last begonia and impatiens need potting now, or tomorrow they will be dead.

Knowing that we, too, will perish, we seek to take care of legal matters while we can. Friends who have terminal cancer have made sure they have a will, a living will, durable power of attorney for health care, and power of attorney for financial matters.

I have taken care of most of this business, but I lack the power of attorney for financial matters, which a friend just brought to my attention last week. I've called the lawyer to make an appointment.

Hopefully, the "frost" won't fall on me for a long time, but stories of friends who had sudden fatal auto collisions have lit the fire under my intention.

Let's act as though the frost is coming tonight.

photo credit: KinoshitaOsamu / iStock

PLANTING GARLIC NOW

Now is the time to plant garlic. It needs about six weeks to establish its root system before the ground freezes, but you don't want to plant too early and allow the garlic an opportunity to sprout.

Choose the largest heads from this year's garlic crop. This is the hard part. Those best, fattest cloves are going into the ground, not into a soup or spaghetti sauce, nor into the oven for roasting. Let the best go in order to multiply next year's crop.

Wouldn't we rather keep the best for ourselves and give away our ratty-tatty stuff? Wouldn't we rather keep the new and give our used stuff to a thrift store or the church rummage sale?

The highest form of generosity is raja (think: maharaja), or kingly, giving. Queenly giving gives open-handedly, open-heartedly, and even without letting anyone know where the gift comes from.

In the case of garlic, we are giving to ourselves. Choose the best cloves, plant them, and harvest a king's ransom of garlic next August.

HARVESTING FARMERS MARKETS

Harvest Festivals abound on this long weekend. Every small town around me has at least one. Also, as of this summer, each little town (population 2,000, more or less) has its own Farmers' Market. Friends—whom I wouldn't have suspected—have a booth selling basil chevre and "cinnful" cinnamon rolls. Last week I bought a very local frozen chicken and a bag of pears.

These markets are as much fun as markets have been for centuries. They provide a chance to visit with friends and acquaintances while listening to live, toe-tapping music that plays in the background. Sweets and savories are sold at two or three booths. Then there's the Thai food booth—red curry, green curry, or fish curry—as well as Mexican tamales and burritos.

Wise livelihood is one step on our spiritual path. By supporting our (usually organic) neighboring farmers, we enable them to make a living while their locavore food sustains our own lives.

COLLECTING SEEDS

The season of collecting seeds has arrived. Since I love to plant seeds, I also like to collect them. I hunt around the nasturtiums for little wrinkled tan balls that are smaller than peas. I shake annual poppy heads into a bowl, and soon I have handfuls of black poppy seeds that I could bake with if I wanted to.

I make a special effort to collect seeds from the biennial plants I love—lupine, hollyhock, angelica, foxglove, sweet William. I want these flowers to return to my garden, so I boost my chances of seeing them again by nurturing their re-seeding.

Many seeds I simply lay in a nursery bed, because I know they are hardy enough to raise themselves. A few, perhaps those that are new to me, I will start in six-packs in late winter.

What are the seeds that we want to grow in our spiritual life? Patience? Generosity? Mindfulness? Go ahead: Plant your favorite seeds now. Today. Plant the intention. Water daily, both in and out of meditation. Notice the tender sprouts.

May your gardens—inner and outer—be blessed.

THE RACE TO COOK MY WAY TO THE END OF THE GARDEN

I am racing to cook my way to the end of the vegetable garden. Every day I fill my harvest basket. My daily goal is to cook everything that's in it, adding ingredients from failed attempts of preceding days. After all, how do you cook a crisper drawerful of eggplant in one go? I divvy the eggplant into various recipes—Italian, Indian, Thai, Israeli, Lebanese.

In the process of cooking these dishes, I create more leftovers than we can possibly eat. So, I freeze big batches of potato-chard soup, chili verde (made with tomatillos), corned beef and cabbage.

When I leave on retreat, my sweetie will be well nourished. He has almost inured himself to retreat abandonment (as he calls it). Every night while I'm gone, he pulls a container of love out of the freezer and warms it up to nourish himself.

Intellectually, he knows that I return a calmer, wiser person. He just needs a daily reminder of my care and concern for him. And his menu is actually quite extensive.

STOPPED FLOWERING

The geraniums in flowerpots outdoors have stopped flowering. I suspect it's their nonverbal message to me: *Brrr. It's too cool out here. If I can't have more light, at least give me some more heat.*

I'm seeing a 95-year-old hospice client. Her hands are cold, so she has a heating-pad muff to warm them up. She loves to fold clothes, hot out of the dryer. Her vision is so-so. And her mind is mostly gone. She's a sweet woman, and she keeps saying, "I want to go home."

Just like my geraniums.

photo credit: shutterstock

LOCAVORE CHALLENGE

I store trays of garlic, onions, tomatillos, and gladiolus bulbs in my unfinished basement. My sweetie built a rack of open shelving into which I can simply slide the trays. The open-air concept allows me to see when the onions start to sprout in April.

We have an apartment-sized refrigerator in the basement, and that's where I keep my potato harvest and zip-lock bags full of sun-dried tomatoes. An apartment-sized freezer is stuffed with green beans, broccoli, and pesto from the garden. Last winter and spring I held more tightly to the locavore concept, and actually managed to clean everything out by June. Well, almost everything—I have just peeled 50 heads of garlic and stored them in olive oil.

This locavore idea is rooted in the slogan: Think Globally—Act Locally. By eating locally, we can cut down on all the oil needed to transport vegetables from the West to the East Coast of the United States.

Here's the fly in the ointment: The vegetables I can buy seem so much more appealing than those in my freezer. The grocery store has more variety, as well. And even the food co-op, which sells organic mostly local fruits and vegetables, offers a more varied selection than what I have in my basement.

I may subscribe to the idea of Voluntary Simplicity, but how does it taste?

A little local chicken broth adds a lot of flavor to green beans. Grated zucchini turns into blond brownies, heavy on the chocolate chips and walnuts. Put sun-dried tomatoes in the pesto and deplete two storage items at the same time.

Next week: green beans, grated zucchini, some broccoli, and oh yes, winter squash—again. Repeat for 20 weeks.

By April, my sweetie is threatening to throw out the remaining two trays of tomatillos. Quick! Think Mexican. Green chili. Well, there's getting used to the color, but it actually tastes great. Simmer pork tenderloin in tomatillos, onions, and garlic for Chili Verde.

Finally the cellar is bare. I can buy any vegetable I want at the Farmers' Market. But wait! In late April, it's time to pick fiddlehead ferns and wild leeks. Asparagus begins to poke up. I refuse to eat the dandelion green salads I grew up on. Last year's kale re-sprouts in the garden, and has enough tender leaves for two meals a week.

Just when I think I can cut loose from locavoring, the season begins again: Rhubarb, cherry tomatoes, cucumbers. The cornucopia overflows into zip-lock bags, and, now that we're also producing some of our own electricity with photovoltaics, it may soon be time to buy an even bigger freezer!

BLAZES OF COLOR

Up in the high country, the trees are already bare, but here, the foothills blaze with red, orange, and yellow.

The wave of color passes from one area to another as it continues traveling southward.

After months of green, the autumn colors pass by in quick succession, each day gloriously warm in the sun, cool in the increasing shadows. Red-orange leaves against blue, blue sky—my eyes are unable to drink it all in, no matter how long I look.

"Everything I cherish will change and vanish."

At no time during the year is this truth felt so intensely. Change is palpable as yellow leaves dance their last dance of the season, fall, circle gently, and come to rest on lawns, flowerbeds, and sidewalks.

Next comes the more subtle season of red-brown oak leaves and yellow-tan beech leaves.

Leaves crunch and swish underfoot. What was above my head is now below my feet. Green has vanished into red-orange-yellow, which turned into brown.

Everything changes—everything, including our dearly beloved selves.

REPRIEVE

Still no frost. Frost has been predicted every night this week, and it does not freeze. Today feels like a reprieve from a death sentence. A rally during the death vigil. How much longer?

For death is coming to the garden. How could it not? Last evening, I made my last batch of basil pesto. The basil is gone. Well and truly gone.

But today, we have one more day, this day, to enjoy the tender annuals. One more day to pick zinnia and dahlia bouquets. One more day to glean vegetables from the garden.

If you had one more day to live, how would you spend it? What would you do? How would you be?

Attend to this one day. This moment. Now.

GENEROSITY GROWS

My neighbor, Connie, gave me a dozen butternut squash seedlings in early June. To begin with, they looked puny, and then I lost track of them. But enough survived so that I have a couple dozen squashes. So does Connie. So does our neighbor, Whit, who planted only two of Connie's seedlings. We are all looking for winter squash recipes.

Whit's wife, Tonia, took most of their squash harvest to her exercise class, and the women there were very grateful.

Generosity (Connie's) begets generosity (Tonia's). Who knows whom the ripples of generosity will touch next? Connie has already given me some of the squash casserole with sunflower seeds she made last night.

Our actions do not happen in a vacuum. Our actions ripple out to affect everyone around us. What can you share with a friend, a neighbor, a stranger, so that generosity grows?

STILL ALIVE

My garden did not die last night. I awoke this morning to 34 degrees and a clear sky, but no frost. Gardens near me have died. My neighbor Connie's, lower down our road, endured frost yesterday morning.

The mystery of life and death. My garden, my life, goes on. Someone else, an acquaintance, dies unexpectedly. Suddenly she is gone. Gone. Her family is shocked.

Meanwhile, I am still preparing for my own demise. It's time to plant crocus and daffodils for next spring's resurrection.

photo credit: onepony / iStock

GLEANING SEASON

'Tis the season for gleaning. Around here, volunteers comb through fields of vegetables after the farmers have harvested, and glean what's left for the food bank: carrots, potatoes, pumpkins, squashes, broccoli, apples.

I'm gleaning in my own vegetable garden. Gathering the last of the cherry tomatoes, the last broccoli side shoots, a few more tomatillos, and ground cherries. I'm also gleaning pinecones from the woods, because they make such excellent fire starters for the wood stove and fireplace. My little old apple tree actually has apples, so I'm gathering them up in order to not encourage the deer to come and eat them.

We glean what we can from various spiritual paths. Perhaps we are attracted to one path, and, slowly, we gather its wisdom.

We can't rely only on our intuitive sense of right and wrong, because some aspects of wisdom can be counter-intuitive. Nor do we follow traditions simply because they are traditions or because that's the way we want life to be. Instead, we test our path against the results it yields. Do we have less stress in our lives? Are we happier?

Little by little, we glean wisdom from seeing things as they really are.

FALL COLORS

The garden chores have slowed to a crawl. This sunny day is one in which to take a walk in the woods, shuffle through the crunchy leaves, and smell those dry leaves that are now just five or six feet under our noses (instead of fifty or sixty feet up). The leaves are changing color fast now, as chlorophyll production slows to a halt, leaving the yellow color that has been there all along, but invisible to our eyes.

Sometimes, our mind is colored by red anger, green envy, blue melancholy, or yellow cowardice. Meditation eventually calms us sufficiently so that we catch a glimpse of the clearness of mind. That clarity has been there all along, just covered over by the colors of our emotions.

Let's take a walk today and pay close attention to the fall colors.

GLORIOUS OAKS

Some hillsides are now bare of leaves; others remain radiant with the reds and russets and golds of oaks, among the last trees to lose their foliage.

The light is delightful, as the naturally shiny oak leaves reflect and refract the sun's brightness. The late-afternoon light slants low across the sky, illuminating the hills gloriously.

From a distance, the aging forest, the aging leaves are beautiful. Up close, we see a leaf's moles and blemishes. When I take pictures of fall leaves, I see that every leaf is aged with black spots, brown spots, or barnacles. Rather like my aging skin.

Everything is aging.

A CLUMP OF BULBS

While transplanting, I found a big clump of daffodils, already sprouted and ready to keep growing. This "find" provides the perfect opportunity to divide the overcrowded clump of bulbs and give some of them away.

Our lives become overcrowded with busy-ness. One activity spawns another. Every new material item requires some sort of maintenance, such as dusting or washing or finding a place to store the darn thing. Things pile up on top of each other. Responsibilities proliferate.

It's time to divide those responsibilities. Give items away. Hand over responsibility to someone else (even though this is very hard). After a period of rest this winter, you too will bloom.

TOPPING OFF THE COMPOST BIN

The end of gardening season is creeping up on me. To entertain myself, I prep the beds for next spring, when the garden will again become a hive of activity. It's good to do as many of those spring chores as possible *now,* when there's time. It's sort of like prepping for a big dinner party by doing some things days ahead.

I picked up a load of manure on Saturday, and used it to "top off" three bins of compost that had already reached the brim with fall clean-up. Now they can sit and "cook" all winter.

This is the effect meditation has on us. We pile on 20 minutes in the morning, and unnoticed by us, it "cooks" in our mind during the rest of the day. Perhaps we can keep our fingers on the pulse of calm for a few hours. Or maybe irritation stays at bay.

What effect does meditation have on you? And on your day?

WOODLAND WALK

My woodland walk is covered with dead leaves; you can no longer tell where the path is. The beginning and end of the path are lined with big rocks, which point the way. Then what?

Sometimes, our path is not clear. Our daily life becomes overwhelmed by too many things to do.

Mindfulness is the ground we walk on. Mindfulness is *not* one more thing to add to our too-busy lives. With mindfulness, a clearer path opens, enabling us to see every mundane moment in a new way.

Get out of bed mindfully.
Pee mindfully.
Brush your teeth mindfully.
Get dressed mindfully.
Drink your cup of tea or coffee mindfully.
Eat breakfast mindfully.
Walk to your car mindfully.
Feel and hear the crush of fallen leaves under your feet.
Drive mindfully.

That way you'll be safer, and so will everyone else around you.

SURPRISE FRUIT

I visited my gardening mentor Ruth's garden to pick up a white fall anemone, but of course she had lots of other interesting things to show me. Her kousa dogwood tree is loaded with red fruit.

"They're edible," Ruth said.

I picked one of the strawberry-sized fruits and split it open with just a slight pressure. I squeezed the creamy innards into my mouth. Seedy, but tasty. Something like paw-paws. "Wow. Put these through a food mill and you have dessert," I said.

The fruits of our spiritual practice are also very "tasty." A bit of calm, less irritation, less judgment, more kindness, less stress.

And you know what "stressed" spells backwards? Desserts!

MUM MEDITATION

The chrysanthemums on the front step were looking tired, so I planted them in the garden. Ah, yes—the ever-hopeful gardener. Will they survive the winter?

Most will not, but one or two might. My garden is just now coming into bloom with mums I planted years ago. I pick a bouquet, and it lasts three weeks.

Often the late-blooming mums don't have much of a season, but these late October days are lukewarm with temperatures in the 50s, so the perennial mums are smiling.

It's never too late to plant ourselves in meditation. If we get an early start, we may bloom early, but some of us don't get started meditating until late in the season of our lives. Still, our meditation practice can bloom.

photo credit: shutterstock

MELTING, MELTING

My garden has not yet endured a frost, although nighttime freezing temperatures are predicted for later this week.

These warm (for October) temperatures make me aware that glaciers and icecaps are melting. Recently, a Bermuda-sized iceberg broke off of the Greenland ice sheet.

The melting of glaciers into rivers and into oceans raises water levels. Bangkok was recently flooded with more water than it has ever seen. Even the houses on stilts have had to be evacuated.

Change—climate change—is happening relatively fast. Our children will live in a warmer climate zone than we do, and their children in a warmer one still.

Notice this day's warmth and coolness. There'll never be another day just like it.

BEECH LEAVES

The first snow has fallen here in the North Country. And we've finally experienced a frost. This morning it was 31 degrees, which had the effect of freezing the wet snow.

Beech leaves have been beautiful this past week—apple green in the understory, changing to shades of yellow-golden at eye level, topped off by coppery tan above. Now snow encrusts leaves and branches.

The pale-green beech leaves almost fooled us into feeling it was spring, yet now their aging is truly apparent.

Friends in their 60s and 70s, who seem young at heart, nevertheless wrestle with their aging bodies. A 53-year-old friend has terminal cancer.

The end of harvest season gives us the opportunity to pause and reflect on our own end of season as wintry frost creeps up on us.

WHEN WE CAN'T SEE THE FOREST FOR THE TREES

Late afternoon found us driving home from Boston in a snowstorm and without snow tires. We found a B&B and checked in for the night. The next morning dawned with a blue sky.

We drove home, observing the spectacular beauty of snow-laden pine trees interspersed with oaks that still bore khaki-green and gold-brown leaves. The contrast was dramatic, and made for a splendid view of the hillsides. I had had no idea of the dense oak population in New Hampshire's forests.

We often can't see the forest for the trees. We are so focused on the thoughts in the mind that we don't notice the mind itself. We "believe" our thoughts and think they are real, when they are but momentary firings of neurons. The thoughts pass quickly. And are gone.

We've had 10,000 thoughts in the past 24 hours. Where are they now?

We've been so intent on the trees (i.e., our thoughts) that we haven't noticed the forest of the mind just being there.

OAK LEAF LESSONS

Oak leaves float down to earth on this last day of October. A breeze rattles them and shakes them off their branches. Earth returns to earth.

We know that last spring, the branches were bare. Sap made of groundwater and minerals rose into the tree and branches, and oak leaves unfurled. Now the leaves, made of earth and water, are returning to earth. Oak leaves are already pretty crunchy, having lost most of the water element that made them glisten red just a week earlier.

Our very own earth element returns to earth, every single day. Dead skin cells, stray hairs, nail parings, poop. The fruits of the earth come into our bodies via our mouths and leave via our backsides. What of this can we claim as "me?"

We walk through piles of leaves, piles of dead leaf bodies. Our compost pile is a heap of dead plant bodies. And the earth we walk on, the dust on our shoes, the dirt under our fingernails are the remains of hundreds and thousands of dead bodies.

Oak trees are baring their secret selves to us now—skeletons against the sky.

And our secret self? Earth, water, air, just passing through.

GROWING QUIETLY UNDERGROUND

I love cold-weather crops. How delightful and how rare to see small green shoots in these days of early darkness. Garlic is the only bulb that's sprouting. Well, the onions that escaped the hide-and-seek of harvest are sprouting, too, but now that they've revealed their hiding places, I may pluck them for a soup or a stir-fry.

Many other bulbs are growing quietly underground. In fact, we gardeners may even be planting some—daffodils, snowdrops, or squill.

As we enter the darkest quarter of the year (October 31 to February 2), what is growing underground in your heart? Perhaps it's time to practice self-compassion.

For some of us, the outer darkness is reflected by an inner darkness, an inner heaviness or feeling of blah. Now is the time to practice the equanimity of "Hello, my old friend, blah." Invite heaviness in for a cup of tea, and just listen to what she has to say. You don't have to believe every word she says. Simply be a good friend. Be a good friend to yourself.

THE SEASON OF DARKNESS BEGINS

In many Latin American countries, *Dia de Muertos,* the Day of the Dead, is celebrated on three days—Halloween, November 1 (All Saints Day) as well as today (All Souls Day). On these Days of the Dead, families go to the cemetery and bring a picnic to party with their deceased relatives. It is believed that the souls of the dead pay a last visit to their loved ones at this time of year, before going underground.

As gardeners, we pay our respects to this season of waning light by planting bulbs in the darkness of earth. There they will grow roots unseen by us during the next several months. In six weeks, Persephone, the mythic Queen of the Underworld, will reign at the winter solstice. Then six weeks after that, on February 2, a little underground spirit in the form of a groundhog will peek out of the earth to check for signs of spring.

We ourselves may have mixed feelings as we enter this season of darkness.

Let's plant spring bulbs now—not so much for hope, because hope engenders anticipatory waiting that is impatient with the "now." Rather, let's plant bulbs to help us notice that gestation takes place in the dark.

Is some aspect of our own lives entering gestation?

APPLE CREATIVITY

The nearby orchards are offering pick-your-own apples at half price. Quick now! Before more hard freezes turn the fruit to mush. In fifteen minutes, I've picked half a bushel of Macouns and Jonagolds. The apple-picking was an excuse to be outdoors on a beautiful fall afternoon.

Now to the cooking and storing of the apples, as I return home with my bounty. What to do with all these beautiful apples?

Fried apples—in butter with a drizzle of maple syrup or brown sugar, and a good salting—remind me of fall breakfasts when I was growing up. Applesauce is easy, and my sweetie adores it.

That still leaves a nearly-full bag of apples sitting in the cold, dark garage awaiting more creativity. Apple cake? Apple butter? Apple pancakes? Or, if I just don't have time, maybe I'll feed them to my neighbor's chickens, and pick up a dozen eggs while I'm there.

photo credit: shutterstock

A SMALL PROTECTED SPACE

My neighbor Connie uses four bales of hay to create a makeshift cold frame. She places the bales so that they form a rectangle, and sows her lettuce and spinach in that small protected space.

In meditation, all we need is just such a small protected space—a single chair. When I visit friends who meditate at their homes, I'm sometimes amazed at their meditation spaces. A few people have an actual room (usually quite small). Others, a chair, maybe a slightly out-of-the-way chair, a chair that you walk by all day long, but early in the morning, or in the evening, that's the designated space where a meditator finds respite from the worldly winds that blow.

ALYSSUM STILL BLOOMS

Alyssum is still blooming along the edges of several walkways. Its delicate white flowers continue to mark the garden pathways, even though it's November. Even though we have had hard frosts of 20 degrees. Even though it's dark out there. Alyssum is a real trouper.

In April, I bought several big packets of alyssum seed. Then I walked along the paths through the gardens, and sowed. By June, the seeded ones had caught up with the ones that came from six-packs. And now, in November, when all the other annuals have given up the ghost, alyssum still flowers. Alyssum soldiers on through the dark and difficult times, and emits a light, bouncy joy with its soft tiny white flowers. By this time of the year, it has spread into a little community.

THE WINTER GARDEN

The winter vegetable garden abounds with bok choy, kale, mustard greens, arugula, parsnips, and leeks. In the basement, at the ready, are just-harvested butternut squash, onions, garlic, tomatillos, and Jerusalem artichokes.

The winter of our lives is fresh for the harvest of wisdom. No longer are we a hot tomato, nor perhaps cool as a cucumber.

Now, with equanimity, born of seeing things as they really are, seeing life as it really is, we can relax into the unfolding of life. Precious life.

photo credit: cyclotimia / iStock

FILLING OUR MINDS WITH MINDFULNESS

Last week I cut down a seven-foot-tall stand of Jerusalem artichokes. The three-by-three-foot patch, with its sunflower-like blooms, was beyond crowded. This week I filled three grocery bags with the sweet tubers that are knobbier than potatoes.

I gave small bagfuls to the carpenter and two neighbors. Now it's time to get creative with recipes. Last night, hash browned; today, mashed. Tomorrow, in soup. Then there's eating them raw in a salad and enjoying their water-chestnut-like crunch.

This week, I finished teaching two classes of Introduction to Insight Meditation. I'm delighted to see how mindfulness has rooted itself in people's lives, whether or not they've managed to establish a formal meditation practice.

Over the course of seven weeks, we practiced

- mindfulness of walking (perhaps with the dog),
- mindfulness of standing (in line at the grocery store, or at the kitchen sink),
- mindfulness of lying down (a body scan while awake in the middle of the night),
- mindfulness of driving (by practicing loving-kindness toward other drivers),
- mindfulness of eating (probably a snack), and
- mindfulness of a daily activity, such as showering or walking through a doorway.

By enriching/filling our days with mindfulness, the mind calms down and leaves little space for worry and anxiety, nor much space for obsessing.

I love to give away bagfuls of mindfulness.

THE GIFT OF NOVEMBER

Now that leaves are gone, the low-slung autumn sun shines clearly through the trees. It's time to take a walk in the woods.

Our vision is unobstructed: We can see clearly through the crowded city of trees, our view unhampered by leaves, which instead of greening above and around us, crunch brownly and noisily under our feet.

November pulls back the curtain. Can we see our lives more clearly, with fresh eyes? Just as we see the structure of trees, can we also begin to glimpse the structure of our lives?

The light of day hurries southward. The "light" of our eyes dims to indistinctness. Yet our inner vision becomes clearer than ever, now that we can finally see clean through our lives.

THE SEED OF STRESS

The stonemason came yesterday to build a step in the terraced garden. I say "terraced" because that is how I imagine this hillside, but so far only a partial terrace exists. Two more terraces await their definition by stone.

I hired this stone man in June and imagined that I'd have a completed project by the end of July. He finished a ten-foot-long stone retaining wall in September, and yesterday, he talked about returning in the spring to do some more work on the hillside.

Do you hear the stress and frustration of this gardener? Weekly phone calls to the stonemason have brought his big silver Chevy truck into our driveway. We see him for an hour or maybe two, and then he's gone. Next week, another phone call.

No matter which way I turn, stress awaits me. Fire him? Call him every day? Find a new stonemason? Forget the project? Do it myself? Let him proceed at his own pace?

I want things to be different than they are. This is the seed of stress.

GARDEN CHARD

My sweetie picked the last of the chard for dinner last night. Well, maybe the next-to-the-last. A few shivering chard leaves remain in the garden.

Chard sautéed with onions and garlic, also from the garden, delights me. I en-joy it. A home-cooked meal—in all senses of the word—makes me happy. These feelings of delight, joy, or happiness are whole-some feelings. Nowadays, researchers call them positivity.

Increasing positivity is good for your mental health. Eating garden chard is good for your phys-ical health.

That makes me happy. And now we're on a positive feedback loop. Happy. Happy. Happy.

photo credit: shutterstock

SMELLING THE ROSES—AND THE MANURE

I drove to the local farm yesterday to pick up a load of manure so I can top off my compost bins. Putting the gardens to bed requires cutting down a lot of dead plants and filling up a lot of compost bins. I have five bins that are filled to the brim with greenery and brownery. Now I can put the brown icing on these squares of green/brown "cake"—about a foot of manure on top of each one.

This is called putting the compost bins to bed for the winter. The dark time of year has arrived. While the world may rush on around us, we don't have to rush to come up to speed. Let's slow down and smell the roses—or the manure. Let's rest in the present moment, and taste a second of peace.

COMMUNING WITH THE MOON

Sixty-five degrees yesterday afternoon—warm enough to carry an afghan out to the hammock and take a nap after lunch under a blue sky, the leafless trees all around me. Mid-afternoon yielded a gentle rain that cleared up in time for the full moon to rise.

I have a hot tub, partly to lure me outdoors on just such a night of bluish moonlight. The moon rides high in the sky now, as if to compensate for the sun that sinks farther south every day.

Night is a deliciously quiet time to commune with the moon and with its current companion, Jupiter. Veils of thin lacy clouds drift across the moon's face as trees reach their bare limbs skyward in silent gratitude.

As I watch the sun and moon, clouds and stars, calm and contentment arise.

UNDER CONTROL. OR NOT.

For the first time in six months, my gardens seem to be under control. Not since mid-May have I felt that the gardens were going in the direction *I* intended. The plants knew where they were growing—kale outside the garden fence (how did it get there?), onions overrun by tomatillos, artemesia popping up again after I had weeded it out of one flowerbed. I wanted *my* plants to grow where *I* wanted, not where they wanted.

How often do we try to wrestle our world into the way we think it should be? The flowerbed would be prettier if.... Our children would be happier if.... We would be happier if.... And this country would be better off if....

Sometimes, we can muscle our world into congruence with our wishes. At other times, all that effort leaves us panting. Sometimes, the world and the garden go their merry ways, no matter how much pressure we apply to change the direction.

Occasionally, I end my meditation with a "prayer" that helps me find some equanimity with the things I cannot control:

May I see things as they really are.
May I see and accept things as they really are happening.

COLE CROPS FOR THE COLD SEASON

The *Brassicas*[3] are the only crops remaining in my vegetable garden—a couple of cabbages, a row of turnips, two rows of Brussels sprouts that have failed to "sprout," three varieties of kale, and mustard greens. I harvested one head of broccoli this year; the rest failed to thrive.

These "cole" crops form the backbone of the fall garden. *Kohl* is the German word for cabbage; thus, we have "cole slaw." The cole crops like cold weather.

What will we have to harvest at the end of our lives? Some kindness, some mindfulness. And perhaps a few other qualities failed to sprout or take root?

Let's meditate now while our growing season remains vibrant. The change of season comes all too soon.

Meanwhile, I'm mindfully cooking up a batch of cabbage soup today to ward off the cold.

---

3 *Brassica* comes from the Celtic word *bresic* meaning "cabbage."

photo credit: pastuslm / iStock

PRUNING THE FORSYTHIA

Those sneaky forsythias entice us with their first-of-the-spring yellow blooms. Then they melt into the background greenery for seven months, sending out new roots and branches. A single bush becomes an ever-widening mound.

Today is a good day to prune that forsythia. Actually, I'm going to rip one out entirely. I don't expect to win. This is just the first round in a campaign to control a single multiplex of forsythia.

Just as too much forsythia crowds the garden, too much stuff clutters our lives. It's time to wade in and prune. Today, I'm passing along my grandmother's crocheted afghans. I'm keeping two, and giving four to my nieces. Then one drawer will have space.

Ahhh. Beautiful space. Now I can breathe.

THE SEDUCTION OF BEAUTY

Driving on the interstate, I see a stretch of brilliantly colored leaves—a rarity here in late fall. The quarter-mile edging turns out to be burning bush (*Euonymus alata*), which has become an invasive in the woods. Oh, my. It certainly is beautiful, but I'm sure no one planted it there, at the edge of the woods and highway.

Then I pass a cliff face made festive by bittersweet scrambling up and down it. A friend recently offered me some bittersweet from her yard. "Yes," she said, "I know it's invasive, but it's *so* pretty."

"And it's illegal to transport it," I said. "Because what are you going to do with it next spring? Throw it away. Where? In your compost pile so it can sprout somewhere in your garden a year or two later?"

Oh, the seduction of "beautiful" invasive plants—and of beauty itself. I'm thinking of those advertisements that feature a beautiful woman draped over or around an item of merchandise, seducing us into buying high-end cars, watches, even alcoholic beverages. Then we read in the news about men who smash their promising careers (usually political) by chasing after a young beauty.

And do we smash our honorable intentions of harmlessness by rationalizing, "Oh, it's so pretty. Just this little bit won't hurt"?

MULCH YOUR MIND

My neighbor Connie borrowed my truck to pick up some mulch hay. We both put our vegetable gardens to bed by covering them with a heavy quilt of hay.

I know. Hay = weed seeds. It takes a leap of faith to willingly cover the garden with hay after spending the summer pulling weeds. But I converted to the Ruth Stout method several years ago, after watching a 1977 video in which 92-year-old Ruth demonstrates how to *Have a Green Thumb Without an Aching Back*.

Our spiritual practice requires leaps of faith as well. I am not talking about blind faith—believing in something without questioning it. I am talking about a more tested faith: You try an approach to meditation with good intentions. After a while, you evaluate your effort. Did it pan out? Did it pay off? Was your faith verified by your experience?

Mulching with hay in both fall and spring keeps the weeds down in the vegetable garden.

Can you mulch your mind with meditation today?

FROST FLOWERS

Now that morning temperatures are below freezing, we are seeing frost flowers. Here's how they form: Moisture from plant stems freezes upon contact with the air, forming ribbons of ice, ice needles, or other frosty forms. Frost flowers disappear quickly once the day warms—and their season is short. It occurs after the first frosts and before the ground freezes solid.

Frost flowers are a spectacular November phenomenon here in the North Country.

So, too, many people in the November of their lives continue to flower. Seventy-eight-year-old Bill still plays piano concerts. His 93-year-old friend George took up jogging at age 80. Eighty-eight-year-old Trudy teaches painting at two nursing homes. We look to these stellar people as role models. *I want to be like* that *when I grow old.*

How will you flower in your old age, when the body creaks and complains? What talent or passion or service will extrude from your life?

FRAGRANCES—SHARP OR SWEET

I'm "planting" paperwhites in shallow bowls filled with white rocks. I prefer the *Tazetta* variety (also called Chinese Sacred Lily) to the more common *Ziva*. Tazetta has a sweet tropical fragrance, but produces fewer blossoms.

So how do you decide which paperwhites to grow? More flowers or fewer? A "sharp" smell or a sweet smell? Doing what everyone else does (Ziva) or something more unusual (Tazetta)?

In our daily lives it's so easy to mimic what others are doing without really paying much attention. Think of how new words come into our vocabulary. Also, gestures, attitudes, and opinions. Do you ever find yourself expressing an opinion you heard someone else say, and then realize that you don't really know whether that *is* your opinion?

A behavior that is replicated contagiously is called a meme (intended to echo the word "gene.") What is the "fragrance" or "taste" of a contagious behavior? Sharp or sweet?

This is the reason why our spiritual friends are so important to us. We want to "catch" their behaviors of kindness and mindfulness. That's the meme we want to remember.

THE CIVIL WAR OF KALE

Kale is a vegetable that brings my cooking to a halt. It's such an earnest vegetable. I want a fun vegetable. The thought of "more kale" makes me want to hang up my apron. I am caught on the horns of a dilemma: fresh vegetables are growing in the garden, and I don't want to eat them. Then, too, scavenging in the refrigerator soon loses its appeal.

This is one more way the mind wages a civil war with itself. "I should eat vegetables from the garden." "I don't want to." The mind bickers with itself every evening before dinner, and so nothing gets cooked. "Kale is good for you." "I don't want kale." How long can this quarrel go on?

A reasonable head of cabbage from my community garden plot steps up to the plate. Inspiration strikes! Cabbage cashew chicken. The cooking fire is lit, and dinner arrives on the table.

Whew!

MISSION STATEMENT OF MY LIFE

The gardener is gone. For seven months of the year, several hours a week, she devotes herself to the garden. Sometimes she does the heavy lifting and hauling. Other times she just keeps things looking nice, trimming, edging, weeding. But now, she's worked herself out of a job. She's done everything that can be done—until spring.

Have we done everything that can be done? Of course not! But how about the most important things?

What would you include in a "Mission Statement for My Life"? What do you care about? Family? Kindness? Accepting life as it really is? Calmness? Living your spiritual practice? What are you doing today to help realize your mission, your purpose in life?

The gardens have been put to bed. And the gardener can stay in her warm bed in the morning for as long as she likes, until I call her in early April. For gardening remains central to my Mission Statement.

RHODODENDRON BUDS

The rhododendron buds are fat and abundant. (A rarity for my bushes.) I can't help but wonder how many buds the deer will feast on this winter. How many of those buds will survive into next spring's bloom?

Yes, I've used many deer deterrents over the years, none of which work entirely. So, now I will put my faith in fate. Or, let's say, I'll put my faith in life itself to see how it unfolds.

You might call it laziness. I call it settling in and letting the wind blow through my branches, letting the sun shine through my leaves. Accepting the world as it really is.

Is this what love feels like?

photo credit: Argument / iStock

PUTTING THE GARDEN TO BED

Every person I meet asks, "Have you put your garden to bed?"

I really don't want to say "yes." It's sort of feels like saying, "Yes, my friend the garden finally died this week." I want it to last another day or two, or maybe a week. But gardening chores are few and far between.

This week, we put snow tires on the car, readying ourselves for the winter ahead. I have to face it: the gardening season is over. Done.

Farewell, dear garden.

REDISCOVERING GRATITUDE

The barred owl called for several minutes as I was meditating at 4:00 this morning. "Who cooks for you? Who cooks for you all?" it asked.

My Thanksgiving cooking took a different form this year: I prepared baked goods to be served during the interludes between 40-minute sits at 7:00, 8:00, 9:00, and 10:00 A.M. at the Vermont Insight Meditation Center on Thanksgiving morning.

The cranberry-walnut scones were a big hit, as I had expected, but the kale-apple muffins were *the* big surprise. The recipe came from *365 Days of Kale*.

During our final sitting, I led a guided gratitude meditation:

Begin by practicing gratitude for all the ordinary, everyday things you take for granted: Running water, electricity, your car, a warm home, safety as you walk on the street. All the services: the post office, the bank and the magic of plastic, which so eases our lives. You can think of many more.

Taking things for granted not only kills surprise in our lives, it numbs our delight in life. "Been there. Done that" is an enemy of gratitude.

I can see I need to practice feeling surprise at kale. Wow! You can chop it up in your food processor and put it in muffins and the kale taste disappears. Magic!

BLACK FRIDAY MEDITATION

The ground is frozen and spring bulbs are on sale. Oooh, the temptation is strong to buy those sale tulips. But then what?

Am I really going to pot them up? Am I really going to buy the bags of potting soil that effort would require?

Then, too, the first seed catalogues have arrived. Oh, the temptation to dive into them and start making lists! Can I put them aside for now?

We see something pleasant—and we want it. The actual craving comes and goes, but we don't notice its leaving, only its coming. "I want." "I want."

This Black Friday is an excellent day to notice craving. Your mantra for today, should you decide to accept it, is "I want." Notice how wanting feels in your body. Notice what happens when you walk away from the wanted object. Leave the store, and keep track of the wanting. Notice its coming. Notice when you can't hold on to it any longer, and it crumbles. It leaves. Notice that space. That's the space of peace.

LITTLE WHITE STARS

My jade plant is blooming with little white stars. While this may not be unusual for people (and jade plants) living in zone 9 or 10, my jade plant and I live in zone 5. I didn't even know that a jade plant *could* bloom indoors until I accidentally discovered the secret: Withhold water in September and October, and the jade will bloom in November.

Actually, I don't have the heart to totally withhold water, so I water very, very lightly, just a couple of tablespoons of water once or twice a week.

Renunciation can make us bloom too. It's counter-intuitive. By giving up something, we will have more time, more energy, and quite possibly, more calm. In this season of buying more (buying more than we can really afford?), what would you be willing to give up? One trip to the store? Overeating at one meal? One hour of computer time before bedtime?

What you can renounce with an open heart?

Let's go outdoors and watch the stars shine in the night sky.

ONE LAST THING

My neighbor, Connie, planted thornless raspberry bushes on Thanksgiving Day. I tell you, there's nothing like six inches of snow to get a gardener going on those very last projects of the season.

The snow has insulated the ground and kept it from freezing. So, Connie just dug in with her spading fork. "Well, my fingers did get cold," she said.

And when the first snow falls on our snowy heads, what's the one last project we will want to do?

One of Connie's best friends is dying of cancer. The friend's advice is "Be more present."

Today. It's the only day we have.

photo credit: ljubaphoto / iStock

TULIPS IN A POT

I craved. And I caved.

Yes, indeed. I went and bought those tulip bulbs—100 of them for $25. That was a good deal. However, then I needed to buy two large bags of potting soil for another $25.

Then I spent an hour potting them up. Now I have 15 pots of tulips sitting on the floor of my garage. It's still above freezing in the garage, and it's dark. I hope the tulips will have enough time to grow some roots before they all freeze up. And I hope the mice won't dine on those tulip bulbs before they freeze up.

Have you been counting the stress involved in this transaction?

craving
buying
potting
worrying about the pots
worrying about mice

All for the pleasant idea, the pleasant mental image, of tulips.

LAWN LOVES SLEET

Sleety rain is falling this morning. It's 35 degrees—a raw, wet day. But the lawn is loving it. Suddenly, the grass is green, the flowerbeds are gorgeously green. The moss looks utterly Irish.

Sleet—unpleasant. Green—pleasant.

By accentuating the positive, we actually feel happier. Our immune system works better too.

Let's go for a walk in the cold rain. It's beautiful out there.

photo credit: HaiGala / iStock

BLOOMING NARCISSUS

A minnow narcissus is blooming in the garden. It was really cold for a week, and now it's November balmy in the 30s and 40s. The weather fooled this narcissus into blooming. A friend has seen a lilac bush leafing out.

I love these fragrant Tazetta type narcissus. They are so sweet-smelling that I breathe deeply in their presence.

Some of us are also late bloomers. The conditions may finally be right for us to show our inner beauty and follow our hearts.

Let's begin our mindfulness practice again, now—this is the only moment we have.

GARDEN STATUES

Now that the gardens have been put to bed and the snow has yet to fall, statuary has become the focal point of our yard.

Aphrodite stands modestly nude beside the fish pond, just stepping out of her bath. St. Francis holds birds in his hands along a woodland path. A meditating Buddha sits in the moss garden under a now-bare Japanese maple. The classical musician I live with likes his "young Beethoven," who shivers in his 18th-century jacket beside the front door.

The center of attention, though, is the fear-dispelling Buddha, who stands in the garden near the front door. With one hand raised, palm out, he greets visitors and welcomes me home, day after day.

HOREHOUND SURPRISE

Of all my garden spaces, I love my herb garden best, and horehound remains a special part of this garden.

When I was young, my dad would occasionally bring home horehound candy—an old-fashioned hard brown candy (consisting mostly of sugar, and in the shape of a lozenge). Horehound is a bitter herb used in traditional cough medicines and for upper-respiratory conditions.

A few years after I planted horehound in my herb garden, I found horehound seedlings sprouting nearby. I potted up the extras, but since gardeners here didn't know what horehound was, they didn't take them. I couldn't give the horehound away. This fall, I decided to plant the ruffled gray-green foliage in the white garden. It looks rather nice as an edging. Conveniently, it has small white flowers.

Often we can't "give away" advice about the spiritual path. All we can do is "show and *don't* tell." "Show, don't tell" is not only excellent advice for writers; it's also good advice for those with a spiritual practice. We can act with kindness and integrity, and wait for people to ask us, "Hey, what's that attractive plant growing there at the edge of your garden?"

BABY BOK CHOY-LETS

Baby bok choy are growing in the garden. While I wasn't looking, two or three went to seed, and now bok choy-lets are growing along the seed stalk, which has fallen over and is lying (and rooting?) on the ground.

When we grow sweet little qualities in our inner garden—friendliness, kindness, cheerfulness, self-compassion—we sometimes aren't paying attention when they go to seed and multiply. Then someone reminds me to be grateful for the blessings in my life.

Hmmm. Well, yes, I am. I am practicing taking no-thing for granted—not my sweetie, not my life, and not my checking account. They are here today, but that doesn't mean they will be here tomorrow. Sometimes, change happens very fast. For now, change is happening slowly, and I can pretend that my sweetie and I will grow old together and be comfortable in our retirement.

ABUNDANCE OF WATERCRESS

I picked watercress yesterday. In two minutes, I filled a five-gallon bucket.

Now for the sorting. I pinch off the top one-third of green leaves, and compost the stem and remaining, mostly yellow leaves. I am separating green from yellow, separating a preponderance of leaves from the stem, which happily roots on any damp surface.

We could also separate what's wholesome from what's unwholesome. Just for today, imagine that you are putting your skillful thoughts, words, and actions in one pile, and your unskillful thoughts, words, and actions in another pile.

Uh-uh-uh. No fair beating up on yourself for *having* unskillful/unwholesome thoughts and actions. We are playing the part of an impartial observer here. *Oh! Isn't that interesting?*

Apply the scientific method: be curious. *How did that happen?* What occurred just before that unwholesome/unskillful thought, word, or action appeared?

Meanwhile, I have put about three gallons of watercress stems into the compost. This quantity of green being added to the mostly brown (at this time of year) compost will hurry the composting process along. And that makes me smile.

FROSTY LEEKS

Yesterday morning, I walked out to the vegetable garden and dug up the leeks. The crusty snow had insulated the ground before temperatures plummeted. Now I have a handful of leeks safe and sound in the refrigerator instead of locked in the embrace of frozen Mother Earth. (Temperatures were supposed to hit the single digits this morning.)

Before our unskillful thoughts and actions "freeze" into bad habits, let's dig them out. Oh, it's not easy, trudging through our inner landscape, which can feel bleak.

The sassy comeback can feel so good. Practice biting your tongue. This may lead to less regret. The quick defensive response to blame just hurls a hot potato back at the person who threw it at you. Practice holding the hot potato. (*Ouch! That hurts.*) Practice dropping it.

Keep digging around those unskillful thoughts and actions. Eventually, the ground won't be frozen. And neither will you.

LAST CHANCE

Quick! The ground has thawed for a minute. That is, *if* the ground is in the sun. If it's in the shade, the earth is still frozen solid.

It's your last chance, *your last chance* to plant those spring bulbs that have been dilly-dallying by the back door.

We usually don't know when we're being presented with our last chance—our last chance to see a friend who drops dead a week later, our last chance to say "I love you" to an aging relative, our last chance to hug an acquaintance who then moves across the country.

Life is precious. *This* very life is precious. Taking life for granted is a form of ingratitude. Taking it for granted that things will continue as they have been is short-sighted, and sometimes leads to regret. "If only I'd known. If only I'd...."

We can't know the future. We can't expect the future to be the same as the past. Nor can we expect things to continue as they always have.

Life is full of surprises. Surprise yourself and appreciate *this* day, this person beside you, this last chance to plant daffodils.

THE RIGHT TOOL

The Spear Head Spade is the right tool for planting bulbs in the semi-frozen ground. This narrow, pointy shovel is great for dividing root-y plants, like hostas, which you would otherwise want to take the hatchet to. The spade's narrow blade can break through a two-inch frozen crust of earth, reaching the dirt underneath, and enabling you to dig a hole for bulbs.

I love having the right tool for the job. My shed is full of tools, so that when I'm ready to do a particular job, I can grab the right implement.

The right tool for our daily life is mindfulness. Yes, we also have many other tools available to us—loving-kindness, compassion, wisdom, clarity, patience, and a non-judging mind. Choose the right tool for the job. Let's implement mindfulness today. Now.

SUMAC TEA

My friend Trudy served sumac tea and stinging-nettle soup for lunch the other day. She's a great forager, so her freezer is full of wild things. She sent me home with a staghorn of sumac, the plant's bright red cone-shaped fruit, so I can make my own lemon-y tasting tea.

To make the tart sumac tea, take the sumac "berries" off the stem. Otherwise the boiling water will leach tannin from the stem into your tea.

Sumac are often considered weeds, but I have come to appreciate their short height (eight to 12 feet) and lovely shape as a backdrop to the garden. The fall color of these shrubs is spectacular: the leaves turn brilliant red. Birders report seeing robins and bluebirds eating the crimson sumac berries all winter long.

We all have "weedy" thoughts that we'd like to chop down and get rid of. Sometimes they form the ongoing backdrop of our mind. "What you resist, persists."

Let's love those weedy thoughts. Irritation. Impatience. Lust. Frustration. Procrastination. Name one or two of yours right now.

Then say:

I love myself as I am, irritated.
I love myself as I am, impatient.
I love myself as I am, lustful.
I love myself as I am, _____.
(Fill in the blank with whatever unlovable qualities you think you have.)

THE COLDEST 90 DAYS

December 9 begins a period consisting of the coldest 90 days of the year. The garden has been put to bed, but the ground is still not frozen. You can plant spring bulbs, which you can buy quite cheaply now. But no dilly-dallying about getting those daffodils into the ground. Buy and plant immediately, because you can never be sure when the window will close on this pre-winter interlude.

I have moved out of the fleece of autumn and into the wool of winter. I wear a wool coat and woolen scarves or neck warmers every day now, as well as hats and aging gloves with tiny holes in them.

My brother turned 60 yesterday and lamented that 60 is old, and he doesn't want to be old. I see the 60s as the gift decade, when you still have your health and are also freed from responsibilities, so you can focus on your purpose and passion in life.

The old, cold season begins whether we want it or not. Let's enjoy it for as long as we can. After all, there are some gifts awaiting us a little later on in this season.

photo credit: Pawel Bruczkowski / iStock

THE FROZEN GARDEN

I harvested the last stalk—well, okay, it was the only stalk—of Brussels sprouts from the vegetable garden. The person I live with has officially declared the vegetable garden dead, and left the garden gate open.

"But the deer will eat the kale," I protest.

"Cheryl. It's over," he says.

My grief is palpable. Once more, I argue with what is—and lose. The garden is no more, despite what I want.

What remains is a now-frozen desert of dirt that water cannot penetrate. The dryness, the aridness of winter.

I could start planning for the next growing season. I could loll around in the virtual reality of the mind. Yet that would be to take my eye off the present moment.

The garden gate is open. The garden spirits (four-legged or invisible) are free to come and go. It is cold. I hibernate in my house.

SEASON'S GREENERY

At its December meeting, the Garden Club had all the makings for wreaths and holiday centerpieces. Women with clippers in hand clustered around long tables in a church basement. Candles sat in the middle of evergreens. Swags of pine branches hung in mid-air as the creators looked at them from various angles. Vases of red and white carnations and alstromeria took shape. Santa's workshop was in full swing, well-fortified with holiday cookies.

One friend refrained from making anything. "I'm simplifying my life," she said.

Oh yes. The price of all this artistic creation is paid later. Dry needles accumulate, and need to be brushed off the table or vacuumed off the floor. After Christmas, there's all the dismantling. I spend hours, perhaps days, decorating the house, and then hours un-decorating it several weeks later. I could simplify my life by minimizing the decorations.

Perhaps one candle surrounded by a small evergreen wreath on the table is sufficient.

STEAMED VEGETABLES

In this season of steamed or boiled vegetables, after dinner we are left with a saucepan of water that we know is perfectly nutritious.

From past experience, I can predict that if I save it for soup stock, it will still be cluttering up the refrigerator a week from now. Instead, I let it cool, and after dinner, I water a houseplant with that green bean water, that potato water, that broccoli water.

When we get steamed, or even approach boiling, we can turn that unwholesome mind state into a wholesome one, simply by noting out loud: "Steaming. Steaming. Steaming." or "Boiling. Boiling. Boiling." or "Worry. Worry. Worry." (or whatever your favorite unskillful mind state is).

As we note or label out loud, our unskillful mind state cools down, and we water our daily mindfulness practice.

A POINSETTIA RE-BLOOMS

My poinsettia started blooming in mid-November. What fun to watch the resurrection of last year's plant.

I repotted the poinsettia last spring. Just as I had suspected, the roots were bound by the small peat pot, in which it had been placed as a seedling. I broke open the peat pot and spread the poinsettia roots in potting soil in a slightly larger, plastic, pot.

From previous experience of trying to keep poinsettias alive until the next Christmas, I remembered, there comes a time in April or May when the plant wilts and looks beyond help. Very likely, I discovered, the plant needs not just repotting, but the unbinding of tightly-wound roots.

How do we constrain ourselves? What keeps us knotted tightly and prevents us from living our authentic life? Self-judgment, self-pity, self-isolation, self-absorption are some of the familiar ways of getting locked into the small world of our own thoughts.

Let's tend and befriend ourselves with loving-kindness and compassion. It's not selfish to begin by sending loving-kindness and compassion to ourselves. It's like putting on our own oxygen masks first: directing these positive attributes toward ourselves, we are better able to express kindness and compassion toward others.

Spread out your roots in your own life, so that you can bloom—even in the winter.

WHITE ROOTS GROWING UNDERGROUND

"Baby, it's cold outside."

Even so, white roots are growing underground. I can see this when I go to my freezer in the basement and glance at those 50 hyacinths in forcing vases on the floor. Their white roots are slowly growing in water. The growing tips of the bulbs show a sliver of green.

Since I can't see what's happening with my tulip bulbs in pots in the garage, I have to trust that their roots are growing too. So far, the temperature in the garage hasn't dropped below the mid-30s—perfect for the bulbs, as long as I keep them watered.

Even just a little mindfulness meditation changes our DNA by reducing our inflammatory response to stress. Ease your mind as this stressful season gathers force, and grow your roots of mindfulness.

MORE FROM THE WINTER GARDEN

Since it was 50 degrees yesterday afternoon, I went to my community garden plot and pulled a few turnips. I also harvested the last three stalks of Brussels sprouts. And I cut my only flowering cabbage for a flower arrangement. Really! Isn't it amazing that the winter garden continues to feed and delight?

Some of my friends signed up for shares in a winter CSA (community-supported agriculture) and are receiving biweekly bags of fresh winter veggies. Although the pickin's are slim in the winter garden, I find I am subsisting easily on what I find out there. If I go and look, there is enough for the next meal. Fresh. Really, really local. And no diesel oil is used to transport the vegetables or the vegetable-buyer (me).

One line from the Loving-Kindness (Metta) Sutta says: "contented and easily satisfied...."

I am content with the offering of the winter garden and very well satisfied with a turnip-onion-garlic stew and some braised Brussels sprouts.

SHIVERING RHODODENDRON

Zero degrees this morning, rising to a high of 12 today. The rhododendron leaves are shivering, each dark green leaf huddled into itself for protection against winter's cold.

Rhododendron leaves droop to vertical and curl into cylinders, a sort of leaf icicle, as the temperature drops below 20 degrees Fahrenheit. The shrub is stressed, but it has developed this tolerance in order to survive the winter.

How do we handle our stress? Do we curl into little balls? Droop around the mouth and eyes? Go ahead and feel the droop in the body. Feel the curling up.

When the temperature warms, the rhododendron leaves will spread their leaves to horizontal and bloom. And so will we.

THE SUN HAS GONE COLD

The sun has gone cold. Standing outdoors in the sun no longer warms me, although we are having day after day of clear sunny weather. The sun rides low in the sky, and casts long shadows all day long. Since I live in the woods, the bare branches of trees nearly always veil me from direct sun.

Eventually our bodies will go cold too. For the last two years of his life, my father had an unshakeable chill that kept him indoors. He, who had worked outdoors all his life, just could not stay warm. He was caged in his house, longing to go run his horses.

The sun has gone cold and weak. I take a walk in the barren woods, searching for signs of life.

photo credit: Edgie / iStock

THE SCENT OF BALSAM FIR

I'm particularly fond of balsam fir Christmas trees, because they smell good. I walk into the house, and the fragrance permeates my nostrils. I breathe deeply, but within just a few breaths the lovely aroma disappears, as the sense of smell becomes accustomed to that particular scent.

The smell arises. Ahhh! Pleasant. Very pleasant indeed. The smell fades and ceases. Neutral.

Arising and ceasing. This is the practice that the Buddha recommended most frequently to householders. Two thousand five hundred years later, it's still a great practice for this holiday season of so many sights and sounds and smells.

Particularly while shopping, note "pleasant," "pleasant," "pleasant." How long does one pleasant last before it ceases? How long does the attention remain on "pleasant" before it starts to wander?

Look closely at this phenomenon during the next holiday party you attend or the next Christmas card you open. Pleasant. Pleasant. And then?

A WILD CHRISTMAS TREE

In late November, the tree service came and cut the tops off three hemlocks that were beginning to block our view of the near distance. I dragged the crown of one up to the house, and Bill cut off the bottom four feet. The green-needled branches still stretch for the sunlight, but now the treetop is based in a red-and-green Christmas tree stand.

The spaciousness among the branches of this wild tree allows us to see the decorations hanging in thin air, much as mindfulness enables us to notice the—sometimes very small—spaces between thoughts that consume our attention. What we assumed was a solid background of constant thinking turns out to be flashes separated by space.

I love having a tree from our own woods living indoors with us. Covered with lights, it reminds us of a sun-blessed greener season.

SIMPLE GIFTS

This is the time of year when I usually buy a bouquet every week or two for the kitchen table. But this year, I'm putting jars of cuttings on the table and finding them to be attractive little nosegays.

One jar of velvety coleus cuttings, one jar of magenta *Iresina*, and another jar of pink begonias. Pretty soon, the collection looks like a bouquet. A welcome sight on these winter evenings when the sun goes into hiding at 4:15 P.M.

You could say I'm locavoring my own bouquet. My "flowers" weren't flown thousands of miles. They came from 20 feet away, from the houseplants in my solarium.

Simple living. Simple gifts.

WINTER

EXTREME DARKNESS

Today is winter solstice—a day of extremes—the shortest day, the longest night. The year has slipped away, never to return. Our life is slipping away. One year: Gone.

Shall we take the hedonistic approach and "eat, drink, and be merry"? Shall we consume as much as our pocketbooks and our consumer society will allow? Or does that feel like "empty calories"—full of stuff, stuffing ourselves and our homes, an approach that leaves us dissatisfied and empty?

In the Middle Ages, some people thought they could attain heaven by self-mortification. Today's young women mortify their bodies with anorexia, binging and purging, and cutting.

These are the extremes: hedonism and self-mortification.

But let us consider The Middle Way, a path of moderation advised by the Buddha. In this time of extreme darkness, how might we eschew self-judgment ("I'm so bad.") and ego-tripping ("Look at me! Aren't I great!")—and instead practice The Middle Way?

"Be a lamp unto yourself," the Buddha said. In these days of darkness—external or internal—notice your inner light. Sit. Meditate—if only for five minutes.

Notice the flicker of kindness in your heart. Fan that ember so that it glows through the front of your body. Spread that feeling of goodwill through the back of your body. Spread it through the right side of your body. Spread it through the left side of your body.

Sit. Feel the body filled with kindness.

SOLSTICE BONFIRE

For years, my sweetie and I have celebrated the solstice with a party attended by friends and neighbors. Always, the challenge is how to move a convivial gathering out of our cozy candlelit house, into winter coats and boots, and down the driveway to the solstice bonfire.

This solstice day, rain began in mid-afternoon—a cold, raw rain—but the forecast showed a few breaks in the clouds. I kept my ear tuned to our metal roof, and at 6:45 P.M., after it had already been dark for two hours, the pitter-patter stopped.

The fire signs (two Leos and one Sagittarius) dashed out of the house into the dark with paper, kindling, and matches. We didn't want the influence of any water signs (Pisces, Cancer, Scorpio), thank you very much.

Within minutes, the fire blazed, and we invited the rest of the party outdoors for smudging with sage, pomegranates (a la Persephone), and anointing.

The solar year dies. Now the sun begins its long trek north again. The large brush pile, which became a corpse of glowing embers, also died.

Meanwhile, we sang and talked for an hour outdoors before I felt the first raindrop, which died its raindrop death on my cheek, where it became running water.

Winter begins.

WINTER RALLIES

The second full day of winter feels like the first day of spring. Temperatures are in the 40s. Dirt roads are slightly muddy. A dusting of wet snow melts as soon as the sun hits it. There are blue skies. And chickadees sing.

Where am I? Out in the vegetable garden, picking bok choy, mizuna, and red Russian kale. Okay, and maybe some Johnny-jump-up flowers for the salad.

This seems like winter in the Pacific Northwest: fall followed by a cold snap, maybe a dusting of snow, and then a spring that ever so slowly unwinds from the end of January into May. But here in the North Country, we do not have the moderating influence of the Pacific Ocean. We are at the tail end of Alberta clippers, the winds that come sweeping down the plains, and the snows that are born out of the Great Lakes.

So far, winter is only teasing us with almost-cold and almost-snow.

As a hospice volunteer, I know that sometimes a dying person rallies when she knows her loved ones are coming from far away. All of a sudden, she looks pretty good, and maybe she's actually eating too. The loved ones think *Maybe she's not on her deathbed, after all*. But a day or two passes, the rally ends, and the dying person sinks, perhaps into a coma.

Winter is rallying now. She's looking very good. Haggard and barren, yes, but also somehow young.

Simply live this day.

RECEIVING SOMEONE ELSE'S GENEROSITY

On Christmas Eve, I volunteered to be the "inn keeper" at a homeless shelter housed in a local church, outside of which stood a nativity scene. I signed up for the 1:00 to 7:00 A.M. shift, and this seemed exactly the way to celebrate Christmas Eve. I felt quite joyful, even though a few of the men sleeping on the floor smelled rather like a manger all by themselves.

Driving home on Christmas day, I marveled at the pink and powder-blue dawn sky. I stopped at the branch of a local bank (in a building materials store) that opens at 7:00. I was probably the first customer of the newborn day.

"Take a poinsettia home with you," Jane, the teller, offered. "We're giving them away to our first 25 customers."

"Perfect," I said. "We don't yet have a poinsettia at home."

'Tis the season of giving and receiving. Receiving the gift of another person's generosity.

I would not have chosen a peach-colored poinsettia named DaVinci. But the object is not the point.

Graciously receiving a gift allows the giver to experience her own joy. And that too is a gift.

CHRISTMAS GIFTS

One year my red Christmas cactus actually bloomed on Christmas day! And a white amaryllis opened. And then I found an orange and blue bird-of-paradise!

Since my sweetie and I no longer exchange gifts, these blooming flowers felt like gifts to me.

Not giving gifts to my loved ones has greatly reduced my holiday stress. Imagine that! After all, a gift is really a way to say "I love you." And we can do that by sitting on the sofa together, looking at the Christmas tree, and all the blooms around it.

Try it now. Sit down with someone you love today. Just sit together quietly, and practice the generosity of love.

photo credit: L_Shtandel / iStock

A THOUSAND MILES OF SNOW

Friends who live in Michigan drove to New England for the holidays. A thousand miles of snow disappeared when they came down the mountain into town. The snow stopped at the town border. People around here have all marveled at the one-month delay in snow. We had a tan-and-brown Christmas. My car was so dusty, you couldn't read the license plate.

Until now.... This morning a foot of snow has fallen. The White-Christmas season that we dream of has arrived.

The gardens and all the undone garden projects are now hidden under a blanket of white. This is the beautiful death of the old year.

White stillness lies upon the land. May we relax our busy-ness long enough to notice the exquisite quiet that underlays the workaday mind. For we have truly entered the land of snow and ice, a place that requires equanimity.

THE END OF BULB PLANTING

Three inches of snow in December means bulb-planting season is officially over. The opportunity for planting flowers that will bloom in the new year is gone. The ground may not be (too) frozen, but how can we see where to plant the bulbs?

What are the wholesome intentions you'd like to plant in your life before the snow falls?

Sometimes we get snowed in by our bodies before we're ready. Wait! Wait! There was something important I wanted to do! Every winter the snow delivers its silent message to us—*the winter of life is coming*.

What's most important to you? Family (a slowly changing collection of dear ones. Notice the change-ability.)? Career? Money (ever-fluctuating)? Your spiritual path?

Now, during these in-between days, when busy-ness has abated and the new year hasn't yet begun, breathe. And notice that you are breathing.

LOCAL SALAD

Company's coming for a skiing weekend, and I know they eat a salad with every dinner. When I peruse the vegetable section at the food co-op, I see that all the lettuces come from California. The cabbage, however, comes from ten miles away. In my spotty attempt to be a locavore, I buy the cabbage and leave the petroleum-driven lettuce alone.

Fortunately, the twelve-year-old is game for the challenge of cabbage salad. She chops and dices, and makes her own salad dressing. Yes, there's a yellow pepper from Holland in the mix. What can I say?

The voluntary simplicity of locavoring can feel like insufficiency, or it can feel like a challenge to our curiosity and creativity. "I don't have enough" vs. "I wonder how we can make this work."

The cabbage salad is beautiful and tasty.

BOILING WATER YOUR CHRISTMAS TREE

A 94-year-old neighbor waters her Christmas tree every day with boiling water. By February (*February?*), her tree is sprouting new growth.

Although boiling water sounds extreme, the theory is that trees stop absorbing water because the pores of the stump become clogged with resin. Boiling water melts the resin, and thereby increases absorption.

In dark times, our minds can become clogged with sticky thoughts that stress both mind and our body. The first step toward unclogging these thoughts is mindfulness. Go ahead and write that thought down, because the mind is slippery. Look at that thought. Is that thought true? Useful? Beneficial? Is it really, really true? Is it so true that you would stake your life on it?

Ask yourself: **How does truth feel?**

Truth feels like "Ahhh." "Yes." "Of course." Truth relaxes the sticky thoughts that are gumming up the mind. Truth brings peace to the mind and calmness to the body. Out of that tranquility spring tender green shoots of creativity and kindness toward yourself and others.

THE ICY TRUTH

Two inches of slush froze on tree branches overnight. When the sun shone this morning, the icy trees shimmered like diamonds.

It's cold. It's wet. It's icy. It's beautiful. It's dangerous driving. It's heavenly.

Our attention freezes onto one of these qualities and calls it "the truth" to the exclusion of the others. We freeze our attention into beliefs, and cling to what our minds tell us.

Meanwhile, the ice on the trees is cold, wet, icy, and beautiful. Truth encompasses it all.

THE OLD YEAR IS DYING

The old year is dying. The body of Mother Earth is losing heat. Rivers and streams are freezing.

Yesterday the earth rallied, perhaps because some of her children were coming to visit her. She appeared as young as springtime. Around here, temperatures soared to 48 degrees. Yes, of course, she still looked brown, with a pallid gray sky overhead, but her youthful energy returned for about 24 hours as we remembered how she used to be.

Now she's lost that energy, receding into the numbness of winter as some animals go into hibernation. We, her Earth children, grieve the aging and death of the year we will never see again. We have fond memories, but this year and this garden are truly gone.

photo credit: MikeLaptev / iStock

HAPPY NEW MOMENT!

Today we celebrate the new year. We turn over a new leaf, post a new calendar on the wall, open a new diary. We choose one moment and celebrate the change of a number. Last year we called the present moment by one number, say, 2017; now we call it a different number, say, 2018. It's still the present moment.

We are never anywhere other than in the present moment. The past is a memory, a thought. It is just a thought. The future is a dream, another thought. Because, really, it is always Now.

The body ages, and, as long as the mind keeps track of time (very useful for celebrating birthdays and new years, for instance), we are caught in a cycle of birth, aging, and death.

Take my hand and step outside the whole meshugas with me now, into the Now, where there is no birth, and there is no death.

Happy New Now.

GROWING NEW ROOTS

Cold temperatures keep me indoors, now that winter has truly arrived. Zero degrees this morning: there are a few inches of snow on the ground, and the fishpond is truly frozen.

The only gardening available to me consists of tending the houseplants. I water them and pick off dead leaves. I give several a haircut—begonias, geraniums, and a wandering Jew—and place the cuttings in jars of water so they'll root.

What would you like to root in this new year? Self-compassion? Joy? Being of service? Friendliness? Patience?

In order to root these (or any other) beneficial qualities in your daily life, send yourself your best wishes right now. By doing this, you generate new routes for the neurons and the mind.

May I feel safe. (Feel around inside your body. Does someplace "feel" safe? After a couple of seconds, move on.)
May I feel happy. (Does someplace in your body "feel" happy?)
May I feel healthy.
May I feel peaceful. (Does your big toe "feel" peaceful?)

Repeat these phrases and allow them to percolate gradually into your mind and into your body. By the time my cuttings have rooted, you will have established some new neuronal routes yourself.

FULL BLAST WINTER

With winter in full blast, I have become acutely aware of the wind chill factor. Air blowing down from the Arctic causes already-low temperature to plummet, creating tundra-like conditions. Even though I have a small stand of white pines and hemlocks to protect the house from the prevailing northwesterlies, I can sometimes hear the wind whistling around the corners of the house.

Lying in my cozy bed at night, I hear the deepest wind chime bonging—a reminder to watch the air moving in my own body. Breathing in. Breathing out.

BELOW ZERO

It's ten below zero on this beautiful, cloud-strewn morning. The patrons at the bird feeder have fluffed their feathers until they look like fuzzy balls instead of sleek birds. (And what wind chill do they feel when they fly through the frigid air?)

If I buy plants that are hardy in zone 5, that means they'll survive down to -10 degrees. That's what the thermostat reads today, here in my garden.

I try to buy zone 4 plants that are hardy down to -20. Then I can be pretty sure they will survive the winter in my zone 5 garden.

These very cold temperatures can also have an effect on invasives of all kinds, which have been creeping northward as our climate warms. Ticks carrying Lyme disease are less prevalent in the northern climate zones 4, 3, and even zone 2, on the mountain tops.

Tree pests such as the hemlock wooly adelgid, which will eventually wipe out our eastern hemlock tree population, can't survive below -10. But we need several days of -10, and only this one is predicted.

We try to knock out our bad habits by giving them the cold shoulder, but this cold-heartedness only puts them into the deep freeze of repression.

Warmth is the remedy. Feel kindness for yourself and for the bad habits.

I love myself as I am.... (Fill in the blank with the name of your bad habit.)
I love myself as I am, impatient.
I love myself as I am, cold-hearted.
I love myself as I am, feeling unlovable.

Morning sun is streaming into our passive-solar house, and warming us up on this wind-chilly day.

SOME LIKE IT HOT. SOME LIKE IT COLD.

On the coldest night of the year (so far), I went to the Some Like It Hot yoga studio for a yoga warm-up.

Afterward, I walked into my mudroom and looked at the cyclamen on the windowsill. Some like it cold—cyclamen, for instance. In London, in January, you can find window boxes filled with blooming cyclamen, and maybe a dusting of 30-degree snow.

What's your inner climate when you sit down to meditate?

Really, we are just watching weather patterns blow through our minds. The scorching heat of anger. The chill of rebuff. The rains of grief or sadness. The tornado of too much change happening too fast.

We don't need to have an opinion (or a judgment) about any of these weather patterns of emotions. Just watch them come and go.

As they say in New England, "You don't like the weather? Wait five minutes. It'll change."

CHRISTMAS TREE REDUX

Today we took down the Christmas tree and carried it outdoors. And there we set it up again, in a snowbank, on top of what is known in other seasons as my white garden. Now that garden is truly white—with snow. For the next ten weeks, we will have a tree standing near the front door, sort of defining the white garden with a bit of vertical greenery. Instant landscaping!

We did this while the temperature was still above freezing and the wet snow could be shoveled and then banked around the base of the tree. Two hours later, the temperature dropped below freezing and now the tree and its stand are frozen solidly into the icy snow.

We think of our words and actions as changeable, pliable, melting away on the next breath. Yet, if we repeat the same thought or the same action over and over, the neural pathway forms a rut, and a habit becomes frozen in place. A habit becomes part of our inner landscape, and we start to believe that's who we really are.

Let's watch our thoughts, words, and actions carefully and make sure that they are in accord with our highest intentions. Let's plant mindfulness at the front door.

LATEST SUNRISE

Today is the day of the latest sunrise. Beginning tomorrow, we gain a few more seconds of daylight every morning. Due to the tilt of the earth, evenings already hold sixteen more minutes of daylight than they did on December 7, the day of the earliest sunset.

Beginning tomorrow, we gain light at *both* ends of the day. Glorious daylight.

In our darkest days, we keep practicing mindfulness, sometimes through sheer faith. Then our faith is verified as we see occasional glimmers of light resulting from noticing the serenity of the present moment. In this moment, the mind calms, and a flicker of happiness gleams for half a second. Notice this mini-vacation from darkness.

Could we take a vacation in the present moment? A stay-cation of being at home in the here and the now?

MAKING A LIST AND CHECKING IT TWICE

It's January. It's cold. It's icy. It snowed last night. It's a good time to curl up with a seed catalog, or a stack of seed catalogs, and dream of spring.

But before I go too far, I need to check my inventory. Don't I already have ten half-used packets of bean seeds?

Last summer, I organized my seed packets by month—March (start indoors), April (the cold-resistant seeds that can be sown directly into the ground), and May (the tender crops and annual flowers).

The seed catalogs beckon seductively. *Yes! I want....I want....*

This is a great opportunity to notice how desire feels in the body. Notice the tricks that desire plays on the mind.

Checking my inventory? How boring. (unpleasant) I don't want to go down to the cool, dark basement. (unpleasant) I don't want to make a list. (unpleasant) I don't want to think too hard and figure it out. (unpleasant)

Can't I just open the beautiful catalogs (pleasant) and buy whatever my little "heart" *desires?*

FIRST HARBINGER OF SPRING

In our household, my sitting on the sofa in the evening looking through seed catalogs is a first harbinger of spring. Page by page, possible vegetables and flowers take root in my mind. Papaya Pear summer squash; Russian Banana fingerling potatoes; White Swan Echinacea. Desire strikes again and again, until my order, which will be charged to my credit card, is over $100.

The credit card allows me to ignore the fact that I am putting myself into debt. I am enslaving myself to work for another five or ten hours to pay off this particular debt.

Sense desire begs for more—more tasty yellow summer squash, more sweet-smelling lavender, more beautiful pink gladiolas. The mind pleads for satisfaction. I smile, and agree that I need another treat.

The promise of the garden calls.

CHINOOKS

The wind blew all night long, making us restless sleepers. We assumed it was a cold front blowing in, and yet the morning is (relatively) warm—34 degrees, which even *feels* warm.

Here in the North Country (of New England), we are not accustomed to the chinooks of northern Montana and southern Alberta—the warm, dry winds that blow down the eastern slopes of the Rockies and melt a foot of snow by noon. Chinooks give a mini-vacation from Arctic deep-freezes, and then winter returns, full blast.

Even so, the breath of winter feels warm here now. We could call it the January thaw, although, surprisingly, the skiing is still good (i.e., not icy).

Feel the warm air exhaling from your body right now. Cool air in. Warm air out.

Take a mini-vacation from stress.

The wind in your body is always changing; sometimes it's restless, sometimes not. How is the wind that enlivens your body different from the wind that surrounds you? That wind may be restless, or it may be calm.

The wind is blowing. That is all.

CHANGE OF GREENERY

The holiday centerpiece that I made four weeks ago, at the Garden Club is starting to look a bit stale. It's still green, but.... What? I'm tired of it? It looks like Christmas, and Christmas is gone?

The three carnations "passed" a couple of weeks ago, and were carried out to the compost pile. The baby's breath have dried out, and their color has shifted from white to off-white, but they're still okay as dried flowers.

While cleaning up holiday decorations, I moved the centerpiece outdoors; it now rests beside the ornamental flowerpot of greens and a gazing globe, playing a new role of background greenery, no longer of center stage.

And so life goes. We ourselves look less fresh than we used to, perhaps a bit browner with age spots, perhaps a bit drier. We may no longer occupy center stage, the focus of others' attention. Instead, we have joined the supporting cast—or perhaps become part of the set. It's another change of scenery.

JUNCOS IN THE CHRISTMAS TREE

The birds are loving the Christmas tree that provides my "instant landscaping" outside the front door. I see sleek, slate-colored juncos hiding in the balsam fir, looking for protection from winter winds.

We too are subtly looking for protection as we go through our daily lives. We want to be safe. In an effort to feel safe, we go to familiar places, and communicate by phone, text, or messaging with people we know.

We could simply be safe in the here and the now, in the unk-now-n. Because every moment is new. Really, every moment is unknown. And we are safe.

photo credit: rhambley / iStock

PRUNING

Gay, the pruner, came yesterday to prune the crabapple and the apple trees. Every winter, she just shows up, sometime in January or February, and an hour later, four trees are pruned.

Under her care and guidance, the two old apple trees, which were growing in the woods when I bought this land 35 years ago, have actually produced apples. Our crabapple trees are loaded with blossoms in May.

Pruning goes to show us that less is more. Fewer branches mean more flowers and more fruit.

What can we prune from our lives so that they bear more flowers and fruit? And fewer busy detouring branches? We could have more time for meditation. More calm. More mindfulness. (And maybe more money too.)

I just "pruned" one pile of paper last night. In less than an hour, an area of two square feet was decluttered. Ahhh. That feels good.

MY FATHER'S LEGACY

My father died sixteen years ago, but today is his birthday, so I'm thinking of him. He had absolutely no idea about flowers, but, as a farmer, he knew his grasses, something I do not know. He could identify wheat, rye, oats, and timothy. And he knew alfalfa and the clovers that he cut for hay three times every summer.

His idea of gardening was to plow up a quarter-acre with a small Massey-Ferguson tractor, then put us kids to work with hoes while he went to jog his harness horses. He himself was not much of a gardener, having plowed too many fields barefoot with horses during the Great Depression. But he did like to move earth with equipment of any sort.

And he liked to grow tomatoes and cucumbers. That was his idea of a garden, out behind the horse barn, fertilized with horse manure, and growing plenty of weeds.

Three of his four kids (including me) inherited the gardening/farming gene. The other one received the mechanical gene.

My father is gone now, but the fruit of his actions lives on. Three of us will be starting our tomato seedlings soon.

CHRISTMAS CACTUS IN JANUARY

My shocking-pink Christmas cactus is in full bloom. Hmmm. What to call it? I've heard of Thanksgiving cactus and Easter cactus. Shall I call it Martin Luther King cactus?

The bloom of Christmas cactus is triggered by fourteen hours or more of darkness.

My neighbor, Connie, keeps her Christmas cactus beside the sliding glass door in her basement. Since she's not in her basement at night, her Christmas cactus enjoy the cool dark, and begin blooming at Thanksgiving.

My Christmas cactus live in the solarium off my living room, where the lights can go on and off at any time of day. (I often read before I meditate in the living room at 4:00 A.M. After meditation, I turn the lights on again and write my blog.) My Christmas cactus, like me, find it difficult to get uninterrupted sleep—and they need fourteen hours of it. They don't bloom until after the Christmas tree, with all of its lights, has left the vicinity.

So it is with meditation. Some of us bloom early, some late, and some in the middle. Whenever it is, it's "just right" for us.

BIRD OF PARADISE

An orange-and-blue Bird-of-Paradise is blooming in my solarium, as it does every year around this time. A friend who had lived in Hawai'i for 25 years gave me the plant. It took a few years for it to become root-bound, and then bloom. Why is it that some plants need constriction before they will bloom?

The same can be said of our spiritual practice. Constricting our activities—sometimes called renunciation—enables our hearts to bloom.

By pruning our busy lives, we make time for a meditation practice. By counting to ten *and* being mindful, we are less likely to say something we regret later. And by restraining ourselves from engaging in the latest piece of juicy gossip, we find that people begin to trust us more. Simplifying our lives leaves us more time for solitude and to be thoughtful of others.

Slowly but surely, our life blooms with love, generosity, and wisdom. Paradise is right here.

ROOTING DIEFFENBACHIA

My Dieffenbachia came in a planter when my mother died, fourteen years ago today. Eventually, the plant outgrew its container, so I split it and planted it in separate pots. The Dieffenbachia has limped along, always shedding its bottom leaves, and looking a bit undernourished in winter, but regaining its health every summer outdoors.

This week, I looked carefully at the green-and-cream-leaved plant and saw about 20 sprouts coming out of the pot. I've now cut off the leggy cane-type stems. Half I am rooting in water; the other half in soil.

Dieffenbachia was named to honor the head gardener at the Vienna Botanical Garden, Joseph Dieffenbach, in the mid-nineteenth century.

We honor the memory of our loved ones who have died, knowing that we shall follow them.

"Death is certain.
The time of death is uncertain."

Knowing this, what's the most important thing for you to do today?

WHITE LINES

The Yard Magician came in early July to edge my flowerbeds. I was making an extra effort to prettify my garden, because a wedding would soon take place in my nearby field.

The wonderful wedding came and went. My summer gardens bloomed and ebbed. The fall garden flowered and faded. I stopped feeding the goldfish in mid-October.

Now the winter garden lies low, its green, then brown stalks cut to the ground. Only a dusting of snow decorates the landscape, like a sprinkle of confectioner's sugar on a sheet cake. Bits of snow collect in the edging and the curves, pleasing to the eye, drawn not darker but lighter, whiter; they separate lawn from flowerbed.

The effort we put into our meditation practice also yields results. Perhaps in our busy workaday world, those results are only somewhat noticeable. But when the busy-ness of our lives recedes, when the clamor ceases, we will see the clean line that has been there all along, calling us to contentment with what is.

The Yard Magician's magic is still at work.

THE PERFECT MICROCLIMATE THAT FOSTERS BLOOMING

My variegated Dracaena is blooming for the first time. A first-grade teacher gave it to me seven years ago, after I spent the school year as a volunteer in her classroom once a week, helping children learn to read. That once five-inch plant is now five feet tall, so last summer I placed it beside my front door in the white garden. Its green-and-white leaves added interest to the shady and therefore mostly leafy flowerbed.

This particular plant seems to like to be wet, so I put it in a glazed flowerpot that had no hole in the bottom. Then it rained for 25 days in June and another 25 days in July. The flowerpot overflowed with water.

The Dracaena was so well camouflaged among the variegated Solomon's seal that I nearly forgot to bring it indoors. Then I "saw" it in early October, and hurried it into the solarium. Now, for the first time in its life, it's blooming—a dozen small fluffy white flowers on a stem.

We all need the right conditions for our meditation practice to bloom. Some of us need to be inundated—perhaps by going on long retreats; some, like geraniums, need the soil to dry out in between waterings. I like to meditate in the wee hours of the morning; others prefer afternoons or evenings. I like study *and* practice; others prefer mostly practice; and those with a sporadic practice may obtain deep benefit from studying in a weekly class.

It takes time to discover our own perfect microclimate that fosters our own blooming.

PARTY TIME

Party Time is blooming! The plant's tiny white astilbe-like flowers appear unremarkable against its hot-pink-and-green foliage. The plant is also called Pink-and-Green Joseph's Coat. You'll probably choose one of these names rather than the Latin name *Alternanthera*.

I bought Party Time instead of impatiens last summer, and then brought one plant indoors in the fall. It makes me very happy every time I look at it.

The Pali word *metta* (Sanskrit: *maitri*) is often translated as loving-kindness. Sometimes it is called loving-friendliness or goodwill. Other possibilities include amity and benevolence.

We can choose the translation that resonates with us. Because whichever word we choose, metta makes us happy.

BEAUTIFUL RIVER BIRCH

I recently attended a writing retreat at a New England inn. In the courtyard near the entrance stood three river birch trees—the largest such group I have ever seen. I remarked on their beautiful peeling cinnamon-colored bark, especially noticeable at this time of year.

"Oh, they're so messy," said the innkeeper. The windy, rainy day had pruned a dozen twiggy branches, which were now lying in the snow beneath the birches. Every wind, every rain, every snow brings down more branches. In the spring, the sidewalk is littered with catkins—the tan birch-tree flowers.

When we are full of desire—for a person or a thing or a situation—can we stand back and look at the unbeautiful that comes along with the beautiful?

For his lustful young and middle-aged monks, the Buddha recommended imagining the excrement of the dark-eyed beauties they so fancied. Before he himself embarked on the ascetic path, Siddhartha Gotama had seen the drooling, heard the flatulence, smelled the bodies of the sleeping women in his harem, and become dispassionate about them.

The river birches are beautiful. And they are messy.

NORTHERN ORANGE TREE

A friend who was moving house gave us his orange tree. Okay. Here in the North Country, "orange tree" means three feet tall in a pot with an orange (that is not yet orange) the size of a grape.

I placed it next to my banana tree, which hasn't produced a banana or even a flower in 22 years.

We might imagine what a full-grown meditation practice looks like—a beatific smile on our always-calm faces—when, really, what we have is a very small practice, perhaps just ten or 15 minutes at a time, not even every day.

The fruit of our spiritual life may seem quite small. *Well, yes, I did hold my tongue in that situation. And I was kind to that person in the convenience store. And I did give some time to help a friend.*

We start where we are. The journey of a thousand miles begins with a single step. The spiritual journey commences with a moment of mindfulness. Now.

photo credit: coramueller / iStock

OLD GERANIUMS

The geraniums I brought indoors in September are getting leggy as they reach for the low light of winter. The leggy stems lose their green and become not exactly woody, but definitely "old." These old stems do not root, so when I take cuttings, I use only the young green tops.

My geraniums are of the nature to grow old—they lose their leaves, get leggy, and have long, bare, tan stems.

I too am of the nature to grow old. I lose the bloom of youth; the body spreads horizontally; and the skin spots brown with age. I've lost my ability to reproduce.

Nevertheless, the old body still blooms with generosity, joy, and service to others.

WANTING WHAT I ALREADY HAVE

The garden catalogs are tumbling into the mailbox. I leafed through a spring bulb catalog, and was immediately caught by delicious possibilities. I lingered over *Amaryllis belladonna* (Naked Ladies)—a bulb that lets it spring leaves die back and then unexpectedly puts up a single stalk of pale pink in August. I already have *A. belladonna*, and have even divided it to scatter around other flowerbeds. I don't need to buy more. Exactly what am I yearning for?

For those of us with chipmunks who eat oriental and Asiatic lily bulbs, Naked Ladies are a good substitute. My friend Anne, in Maryland, says that Naked Ladies are a weed for her, springing up helter-skelter in her lawn.

Perhaps what I am yearning for is that *A. belladonna* perform as beautifully as photos would suggest. They are short bloomers, and often gone by before I even notice them. Am I thinking that if I only had more, then I would have more blooms, more pleasure, that I would notice them more?

Life is brief. Everything we cherish perishes. Sometimes, much too soon.

JANUARY THAW

The January thaw has arrived. Drip. Drip. Drip. The snow on the roof is melting, and will soon avalanche off the north side of the house. The front walk puddles between crusts of ice. The glacial shield that has covered the driveway has begun to crack and fissure and run off.

Outdoors, change is visible everywhere. Snowmen are melting; snow forts have collapsed; ski trails are useless. The structures of the season—flakes, drifts, and banks—age and disappear.

photo credit: stsmhn / iStock

NEVER-NEVER PLANT

I love variegated foliage, so four summers ago, I bought a Never-Never plant (*Ctenanthe tricolor*) for the centerpiece of the flowerpot at my front door.

Never-Never's leaf is green and white on top and wine-colored on the underside. That first fall, I brought the Never-Never pot indoors, and by the next spring one sprig had multiplied to a nice handful of starts. The pot went back outdoors, beside the front door. By the third summer, the pot was filled with Never-Never plant, and I began to divide it and use it as contrasting foliage for other annuals. Right now, one pot of Never-Never is nicely accented by the ever-blooming Diamond Frost euphorbia. (Never-Never with Ever-Ever.)

Do you ever swear to yourself: "I'm never, never going to do (or say) *that* again." "Never, never" is our wake-up call to be mindful.

We might consider taking the five precepts, perhaps every day, as a reminder that we really do want to live as harmlessly as possible.

Today, I intend to:

do no harm to anyone
take nothing that is not freely given
use my sexual energy wisely
speak truthfully and helpfully
and keep my mind clear.

The precepts are not a forever-and-ever sort of thing. Of course, we break them in tiny ways all the time. But the precepts assist our intention to live the best life we can.

BLEEDING HEARTS

My hospice client, D, died recently, and I am sending sympathy cards to her husband, her daughter, and her son.

Sometimes I make my own cards, using photos of flowers in my garden. For sympathy cards, I particularly like to use pictures of bleeding hearts. In my garden, I have both the pink and the white varieties.

Death comes to all of us. Sometimes suddenly. Sometimes slowly. I had been visiting D for six and a half years.

Grief comes to those who loved the deceased. D is no longer here. I will not be going to see her on Tuesday afternoons. I contemplate the mystery of "gone." *Gone where?* The mind wants to know. Gone where every other person, animal, and plant goes. Gone where every thought goes.

The mind goes on remembering and asking unanswerable questions, trying to protect the heart, which, if not bleeding exactly, is weeping for its loss.

NOT FERTILIZING YOUR HOUSEPLANTS

If you follow the directions on your houseplant fertilizer, you will over-fertilize your poor plants. More is not better. After all, those who make it are in the business of selling fertilizer; they're not in the business of saving your plants.

Fertilizer should be applied only during periods of active growth, and if you look outdoors, you can see this means not-during-the-winter. Plants in low-light situations (e.g., six weeks before and after the winter solstice) do not benefit from fertilizer. My rule of thumb is to stop fertilizing in November, December, and January. I stop when the spirits go into the earth (All Souls' Day, November 2), and I start when the earth spirits peek up again on Groundhog Day.

Our plants need a rest from grow-grow-grow, just as we need a rest from the go-go-go of our lives, our jobs, and our responsibilities. I have a couple of retreats planned for March, before gardening season begins in earnest.

And you? How and where do you take your solitude? When do you rest your mind? When do you rest your five senses, in order to see in full Technicolor and hear in full surround sound again?

Stop fertilizing your life with more, more, more. More is not necessarily better. We too need a rest period, along with our plants. Sign yourself up for a meditation retreat today.

THE FROZEN THROES OF WINTER

Arctic winds are racking the body of Mother Earth here in the northeastern U.S. After the January thaw, and just when we thought, *Yes, we're going to survive winter after all*, the death rattle begins, and the house shudders.

Outdoors, the wind sounds like a never-ending freight train roaring down invisible tracks a block or two away. The furnace fights the chill, turns on and off and on again, trying desperately to maintain a steady temperature, but the extremities of the house cool down nevertheless.

The house groans as we, its inhabitants, snuggle deeper into rest, hiding under wool blankets, and down, and fleece wraps to protect us from polar gusts.

And yet there are only four more days until the groundhog pronounces winter is terminal.

IS HAIR REPELLENT?

Are the deer eating your shrubs this winter? There are several possible deer deterrents, but today I want to focus on just one: human hair.

I used to think that I should go to the hair-styling salon and ask for their trimmings. Then I realized: I brush my hair every morning. I use a bristle brush, so every few days I rake my comb through the brush and garner a very unattractive hairball. This I place in a 6"x6" piece of net, gather up the corners, and tie with a string. Voila! An inexpensive, homemade deer deterrent. You could even say "made with (some) recycled materials."

My hair is beautiful and bouncy, and I love the daily exercise of brushing it. But what is so attractive about hair? *Not* the hairball that results from cleaning my brush.

What's the difference between the hair on my head and the hair in the hairbrush? They're both long strands of dead cells. The hairs on my head run mostly parallel, while the hairbrush yields a tangle. Is it the orderliness that's so pleasant to our eyes?

We can see that hair, *per se*, is not really attractive. How do you feel about a hair in your food?

Let's tie those hairballs onto our rhododendrons, and hope they're not attractive to the deer either.

LOCAVORE: EATING MY OWN STOREHOUSE

Recently I read *Animal, Vegetable, Miracle*, by Barbara Kingsolver. Although I didn't make a conscious decision to become a locavore, as she did, for a year, I've been much better this winter at using local produce, beginning with the foodstuffs stored in my basement.

It's never difficult to use the onions and garlic. In any recipe that calls for one clove of garlic, I use one head, and I still don't work my way through my garlic supply by July. The onions last until April.

The potatoes require some effort, because the weight-watcher who lives in my house complains about starch.

The pumpkins are starting to show their age; it's time to have my own personal pumpkin festival. Just a few pots of green chili, and I could work my way through my extensive supply of tomatillos (and make a dent in the garlic too!).

Why is it so hard to open the freezer door downstairs?

This winter I have refrained from buying the cornucopia of local vegetables offered at my local food co-op. I simply buy one thing at a time—for instance, this week, one small head of cabbage.

This means that some evenings I have to open the freezer door and pull out a package of home-grown green beans, grated squash, or pesto. I expect I am going to achieve a long-sought-after goal: a nearly empty freezer by June.

All I had to do was apply a tiny bit of renunciation (not buying fresh veggies) and determination (to use the frozen organic veggies I grew myself). These two paramount qualities of the heart are feeding my household perfectly well this winter.

AIR QUALITY IN THE HOME

Houseplants improve our indoor air quality. During these winter days, when our windows and doors are closed tight, it's good to know that we can get "fresh" air from our houseplants. Philodendron, dracaena, spider plant, English ivy, ficus, and peace lily are particularly good at converting toxins from household cleaners and polyurethaned floors.

For the average house (under 2,000 square feet), we need at least fifteen houseplants. Do we gardeners need any better excuse for our indoor gardening?

How about improving the quality of our inner "air"? Particularly the air time that our mind gives to various dissatisfactions—at work or home— including with that "irritating" neighbor.

Plant some loving-kindness in your mind right now. Begin with your self.

May I feel safe.
May I feel happy.
May I feel healthy. (Thank you, my dear houseplants.)
May I feel peaceful.

Send loving-kindness to your nearest and dearest (even if they have four legs). And yes, send loving-kindness to that difficult person.

There's the distinct possibility that you will feel neither loving nor kind. That's okay. This is a practice, and we are practicing.

Go ahead. Improve your inner air quality right now.

GROUNDHOG DAY

The groundhog is going to have a tough time today, here in the North Country. In December, the ground froze into an ice block, due to no snow cover.

When my neighbor Connie wanted to roast some roots for Christmas Eve dinner, she took a hatchet to the garden, because the spading fork just bounced off the frozen earth. (I can vouch that the resulting parsnips, carrots, potatoes, turnips, and caramelized onions were worth the effort; they were sweet and delicious!)

January brought snow, then a layer of ice, another layer of snow, another layer of ice. February began yesterday with several inches of snow, and today there is more snow.

That groundhog will need heaters on his paws and a hardhat on his head to tunnel through the tundra here. Maybe he should just stay in bed. Sleep sounds so much more inviting.

Torpor, or sleepiness, is one of the five hindrances to our meditation. Torpor is *so* seductive. I should know—I have taken many nap-lets on the meditation cushion. Summoning will is nearly impossible as energy drains right out of the body.

I have become aware (= mindful) of the early warning signs of a doze. Here are my indicators. (Yours will be different.)

1) The breath feels like it drops off a cliff. It lets go. (This is a one-second experience, and therefore, easy to miss.)

2) The breath has a four-part pattern. First, a deep breath, followed by a slightly shallower breath, followed by a still shallower breath. The fourth breath is a very light breath, followed by a pause. That pause is heavenly.

Then the pattern repeats.

3) Nonsensical images or phrases arise. I call them dreamlets, because they each last about one second. I think I'm conscious, but the dreamlet is a mini-dream that's just about to ensnare me.

This is the time to stand up and practice standing meditation. But the seduction continues. *Oh, I'm awake now*, I think. *I'll just continue to sit. Z-z-z-z-z.*

HIBERNATING AT HOME

Due to a big snowstorm, all schools and events have been canceled for the past two days. Even though I have a four-wheel-drive truck (for hauling gardening stuff, of course!) and have been able to drive wherever I need to, I have mostly opted to hibernate at home. It's rather nice to enjoy the luxury of being snowbound, and to take the opportunity to renounce the world.

Today I had wanted to go to a Garden Writers meeting in Boston, but I heard that the streets of Boston were flooded (and freezing into ice rinks) due to frozen storm sewer drains. I decided to stay home, rather than go skating in my car, along with a city's worth of other skating cars.

Renunciation is one of the ten paramount qualities of the heart that we practice. After all, practice makes perfect(ion).

But renunciation is *so* counter-cultural—just the word "renunciation" is enough to make us scrunch up our faces, wrinkle our noses, and say, "Ooooh. I don't think I want any of that." (Thereby renouncing renunciation!)

I love these snow days, because they give me an excuse to renounce the world, to hibernate with the Dharma, to meditate and to read, to prune my activities way back, so that in the spring, I can spring into action.

HOT WEATHER / COLD WEATHER

My brother just returned from a vacation in Palm Springs, California, where he saw a little flowerbed that made him think of me. Poppies and pansies were growing together.

Poppies are a hot-weather flower, and pansies are a cool-weather flower. They don't grow together in my garden. Pansies bloom in April and May, and poppies bloom in June and July. But they're both cute, and their colors complement each other.

Sometimes we want both-ness in our lives. We want friends or family to visit, *and* we want our solitude. We want a paycheck, and we don't want to go to work. We want a garden, and we don't want to garden.

Our minds think we can have it all, just as we want. Our bodies act out another message. Still, our mind believes it is in control and drives the body to do its will.

What does your mind want? And what does your body "say" about that?

Palm Springs, a city in the desert, has more than a hundred lush green golf courses. What might the body of Mother Earth "say" about that?

HAPPY HYACINTHS

Five hyacinths are blooming in vases in my basement, and the other 45 are budding. In the past four days, I've given away 20 vases, with a hyacinth in each one. Yesterday, I gave one to my writing group leader, Ginnie, and she told me it was her birthday!

On these snowy days, it is amazing how much difference a single blooming hyacinth makes. All our attention rests on this single flower and its beautiful fragrance. In a few months, we will be inundated by flowers, and we will barely notice them as individuals. Today I am inundated by snow (six inches so far), and unless I am out in it, I barely notice it.

My attention is resting on the blooming hyacinth on the kitchen table. And I feel happy.

photo credit: Dhoxax / iStock

THE HEAVENLY FRAGRANCE OF GARDENIAS

My sweetie's mother—also named Sweetie—loved gardenias. They reminded her of the corsages she wore to debutante parties when she was young, back in the Roaring Twenties.

One Christmas, I gave her a gardenia plant. When she died, in 1995, I took her gardenia plant home with me. It's been limping along in my solarium ever since.

I knew that gardenias like a foliar spray, but I never quite managed to spritz it regularly. Then I found a salmon spray next to the fish emulsion at the garden center, and last month I began spraying the gardenia every day or two.

My sweetie complained of the fishy smell. The label does say it's a "superior *fermented* salmon product." Nevertheless, the stinky smell has rewarded me with a record five white blossoms, which exude a heavenly fragrance.

Sometimes our meditation practice limps along—even for years—before we find just the right nutriment—a teacher, a teaching, or a community (at home or on retreat). Then our practice flowers, and we realize that the heavenly actually resides within us, right along with some of those "stinky" qualities.

MORE. MORE. MORE

Okay. Okay. I have twenty hyacinths that are blooming or about to bloom, but when I went into the farm and garden store for bird seed, there, at the check-out, was a pot of little daffodils for $3.99. An impulse buy.

I brought them home and put them—where? Next to the paper-white narcissus. More is better. Right?

More hyacinths: I have five in bloom today and fifteen that will bloom—soon.

I *need* more flowers. At least that's what it's feels like.

Just yesterday, I was singing the praises of one. Just one. Just a single hyacinth. Then craving struck. And I wanted more. More. More.

What am I hungry for? What am I really hungry for?

Spring.

MORE IS TOO MUCH

Oops. I wanted more. And, boy, did I get more!

I found two hyacinth-forcing vases at the thrift shop yesterday, and as I was storing them away in my vases cabinet, I discovered a dozen hyacinths inside the cabinet, blooming in the dark. Yes, their leaves were the palest green, practically white. And the flowers were stooped over, the flower stalk having hit the "ceiling" of the shelf above.

"Be careful what you wish for," conventional wisdom tells us. Yesterday I wanted more, and, sister, I got more.

What, really, do we do with our "more"? More clothes. More flowers. More food. More knickknacks.

As my neighbor Whit wisely said, when we were talking about a wealthy person's McMansion: "You can only sit in one chair at a time."

We can only wear one coat, one sweater, one undershirt at a time. We can only drive one car at a time. We can only smell one flower at a time.

And the more? More is actually quite stressful. Take a close look.

I can tell you, a dozen bent-over blooming hyacinths are stressing me.

WHERE DAFFODILS ARE RARE

We were on vacation in Mexico one winter recently, and I chuckled to see a particular sidewalk vendor who was selling single potted daffodils, hyacinths, and stargazer lilies. This vendor always sat on the north side of the block, in the shade, to keep his ten pots of flowers as cool as possible. These cold-weather plants are as rare in Mexico as bougainvillea and bird-of-paradise, warm weather natives, are here in the North Country.

It's startling to see something you take for granted, like snow, treated as a rarity by someone else—a visitor from Burma or Uruguay, for instance.

The first step of our spiritual path, according to the Buddha, is generosity. This week, I am giving away blooming hyacinths in their vases. The recipients are always appreciative. "Oh, spring," they smile and sigh.

But once in a while, someone will say, "Why do you do that? Don't you want to keep them? Or at least keep the vases?"

Our spiritual path is all about letting go. Giving with an open hand. Eventually, we will have to let go of *everything*. Even our bodies. I'm just practicing by letting go of little things.

NATURE'S PRUNING

Last night's rain coated all the tree branches with ice. The morning sun shining on the ice-covered branches made the trees twinkle, as if elves had draped the forest in fairy lights. The scene was spectacularly beautiful.

Yet the ice weighed down branches, causing many to break, littering lawns, paths, and roads with tree limbs. This is Nature's way of pruning. Perhaps it reminds us of the need to prune our own shrubs and fruit trees (or the ornamental varieties—crabapples, flowering cherry trees, and such).

We might also consider pruning some of our so-called "bad habits"—irritation, impatience, spending too much, gossiping. You well know your good old friend—the habit that bugs you.

The first step in such pruning is mindfulness. "Oh, there it is." (Begin by pruning off the word "again.") A professional pruner stands back and look at the tree. We stand back and look at our habit in action. "Oh, I'm gossiping now." Feel how it feels in the body; feel the sensations. Listen to yourself; hear. Notice how you feel emotionally. Becoming aware is the first step.

The second step is loving yourself the way you would love a puppy that you are training. The puppy has its annoying habit of barking or jumping up, yet you calmly train your dog to lie down—and you love your pet. Bring this same love and calmness to your own annoying habit. "Stay. Stay. Good dog. Good for me."

The third step is to refrain from the action, while practicing mindfulness of the sensations of the body and the feelings of emotions. Count to 10 *and* notice how irritation feels in the body. Zip your lips *and* notice the pressure of words wanting to come out. Notice the busy mind.

Step by step, we begin to prune our internal landscape.

AERATING THE FISHPOND

I slog through the icy snow on snowshoes today to take a close look at my little fishpond. "Close" is a relative term, since I am standing atop the backs of metal lawn chairs that are completely covered by snow, except for the top inch.

I poke a shovel through the snow and into the three-foot-deep pond. Fortunately, it goes right into the water. Seven goldfish and five frogs are hibernating in the icy water to the hum of a circulating pump, which I turn on for an hour a day, specifically to create this hole in the ice.

What I notice is that the water has no smell. If it's been iced over for too long, the fish use up all the oxygen in the water, conditions become anaerobic, and all the fish and frogs die. Pee-yew.

So far, this winter, so good.

The breath may not seem that interesting, but imagine if you ran out of air. Breathing could become very interesting, very fast.

The breath is such a handy meditation object; it's always available, no matter where you are. It might be worth a bit of curiosity and interest to observe how the breath actually functions.

Today I'm glad the fish and I are both still breathing.

REBALANCING FLOWER POTS— AND MEDITATION

In the fall, I bring indoors the flowering pots that have been sitting beside the front door all summer. In the winter greenhouse, some of the plants thrive—like the geraniums; others limp along or are lost altogether.

Now I'm trying to "rebalance" whatever remains in the big pots. Trim back the two-foot-tall geranium. What to do with the variegated ivy? Shall I swirl the four-foot-long trailing vine around the pot? One variegated impatiens survived, and I'm rooting cuttings of it, because I love its deep-pink double flowers that coordinates with the magenta trim on my house.

Sometimes we have to rebalance our meditation practice. When irritation gets the best of us, we practice loving-kindness. When the woes of the world overwhelm us, we practice compassion toward ourselves. When the mind refuses to settle down, we give it something to contemplate.

In these ways, we rebalance and freshen up our meditation so that it can rebloom.

FROZEN SNAKE

A friend went for a walk in the woods the other day and found a frozen garter snake. What's a snake doing outdoors in February? This one was seeking warmth under a cover of leaves, but during the previous night, when temperatures dropped to 18 degrees, a few leaves did not provide a warm enough cover. A warm sunny day (of 48 degrees) had lured the garter snake to venture out, but the frost that night was killing.

Sometimes a warm, cozy bed lures me into lolling around when I could just as well be meditating. The dark of pre-dawn is an excellent, quiet time for the solitude of meditation. Yes, the house is chilly, but I have my fleece pants and tops all laid out, ready for me to hop into.

When the chill of a killing frost comes to us, where will we find our warmth of mind?

DYED DAISIES

My sweetie bought me a bouquet of daisies at the supermarket. Daisies in my favorite colors, pink and magenta. Dyed daisies.

"Dyed daisies?" he asked. "How do you know they're dyed?"

Well, first of all, their leaves are maroon. And secondly, the water in the vase is now pink, as the color slowly leaches out of the stems.

He felt cheated. I still love looking at this ever-so-vibrant bouquet.

We expect our flowers to be natural, to have the au naturel look, so, naturally (ahem), my sweetie feels cheated when he finds out the flowers have been "made up" to look more beautiful.

I'm very fortunate that he likes my au naturel looks, because my youthful beauty leached away some years ago.

Good looks leach away from all of us. When we're young, we're cute or maybe beautiful. Some people's good looks remain longer than those of others. One thing for sure. We will all wind up just like the daisies. Beautiful today. Faded tomorrow. And then after that, out to the compost pile.

Meanwhile, I can appreciate the pleasure I receive from looking at the pink and magenta daisies. And I can bask in the thoughtfulness and love of my sweetie.

WILTED DAISY. WILTED ME.

One stem of my Valentine's bouquet wilted. When I look closely, I see that the stem had mildew.

Sigh. One stem of daisies became sick and wilted. Sort of like me—I have a drippy cold today and feel better when I "wilt" onto the sofa.

Sickness is a fact of life—for us and for our plants and flowers. We get sick, whether or not we want to. Our flowers become sick, even though we don't want them to.

The Buddha recommends we contemplate this fact of life. Even when we are in the pink of health.

My daisies are pink. And I am wearing pink today. But the pink of health eludes both them and me.

photo credit: R_Koopmans / iStock

DRIED UP

The potting soil that I used in January to pot rooted cuttings was too dry. Almost all the cuttings have dried up and died; I'm so disappointed, I don't even want to write about it.

Now I'm ready to plant the next round of cuttings, and I'm fretting over a potting soil recipe.

My last potting soil was about one-quarter vermiculite, and that was not sufficient to keep the soil damp enough. Now I've bought a bag of perlite, also for water retention, and I'm crossing my fingers, hoping that the new mixture will work.

Sometimes our meditation practice dries up. It seems that it's not going anywhere, and we lose interest. How can we retain interest in this practice that we know is good for us?

Some people switch to a different form of meditation. Some people give it up altogether. I rely on my spiritual friends to keep me in the vicinity; I sit for 20 minutes every day with them. I'm also signing up for a retreat, because retreats usually inspire me.

It can take a bit of creativity to find the "recipe" that's right for you. Add some loving-kindness practice or some gratitude practice to get the juices flowing. Or do mindful movement or walking meditation instead of sitting meditation.

The key is to bring mindfulness to this very moment. Even this very unsatisfactory moment.

SUMAC TEA—HIGH IN C

My friend Trudy gave me a staghorn of sumac two months ago, and I use it to make sumac tea, which is high in Vitamin C. Just the remedy for my drippy nose.

The flavor of sumac is almost lemony, and the color of the tea is pink. I'm drinking my sumac tea hot; I'm drinking it cold; I'm using it to flavor fizzy water. Hydrate. Hydrate.

Thanks to the generosity of Trudy, I can enjoy this cold remedy from the wild.

TAPPING INTO HAPPINESS

With daytime temperatures above freezing and nighttime temperatures below freezing, the sap is starting to run. It's time to tap the sugar maples.

My spiritual friend, Vera, has tapped 22 trees in her yard this month. My farmer-neighbor taps 147 trees on my property, and thousands more on his own. Forty gallons of sap boil down to produce one luscious golden gallon of maple syrup.

Sometimes, it takes forty years of life for us to dare to distill ourselves into the person we want to be.

My life began anew at forty, when I followed my bliss and wrote my first book. For my friend Trudy, life began at sixty, when she left an abusive marriage.

Do we just let dissatisfaction boil our lives away? How do we finally tap into sweet happiness?

There are two kinds of happiness:

- *Surface Happiness*—when we get what we think we want, and
- the *Deep Happiness* of contentment with life, regardless of our outer circumstances.

A first step to finding deep happiness is to practice gratitude every day. Notice, really notice the people, things, and situations in your life for which you are truly grateful.

Sweet.

YEARNING

The houseplants are all leaning toward the sun. They look as if they'd jump out of the window, if they could. I can practically hear them saying, "Let me out. Let me out of here." They are yearning for the sun.

We too yearn for something, perhaps something we can't quite put our finger on. We are hungry for Truth. I don't mean "truth" as opposed to "lies." We are looking for something genuine, something authentic.

We busy ourselves pursuing the things we think will make us happy: children, money, career, family, marriage, clothes, flowers, gardens. Our lives are filled with busy-ness, with busy pursuits, some of them good. Still, the yearning remains.

Oh, days, weeks, years can go by, and we don't notice. Then something, perhaps some little thing, triggers it.

Stop. Come home to yourself. Retreat for an hour, or a day, if you can. I've just signed up for a week-long retreat at the end of March.

FUNERAL FLOWERS

I like to send flowers to the family when someone dies, even though the obituary says "…in lieu of flowers." I often send the flowers directly to the home rather than the funeral home.

I like flowers; I like to receive flowers. So I just assume other people do too.

In order to support local businesses, I go to whitepages.com and type in "florist" and the zip code where my friend lived. Then I call and order cut flowers rather than an arrangement.

I try to remember the death date, so I can send flowers again on the anniversary of the death. The rest of the world may have mostly forgotten the dead person, but the family re-members.

Funeral flowers remind us of the impermanence of life. One day, one year, we are in full bloom. A few days or years later, we start to wilt—and finally we face death and the decomposition of our bodies.

Flowers don't have person-hood, so we can easily see how decaying compost gives rise to new life. When it comes to people, though, our attachment to person-hood, to "self," interferes with this simple, straight-forward understanding.

A friend who had a heart attack and a near-death experience said she looked down at the carcass on the table—the carcass she had formerly called her "self."

How are our physical bodies really any different from flowers?

THE CURLY HOSE

Last fall, my sweetie brought home a curly hose that looks like a giant-sized old-style telephone cord. I had been looking at these hoses in the gardening supply catalog for a few years, but I wasn't sure it would be quite right for my solarium.

Once the automatically-coiled hose appeared in my life, however, I immediately put it to use. But first, I had to buy a faucet-to-hose adapter at the hardware store. The adapter was very easy to install. Suddenly, I could neatly and easily water my 50 houseplants, even the ones that are 20 feet away from the sink.

There's a lot of meditation paraphernalia in the catalogs. How do you decide which cushion? Which bench? Which statue? Which shawl? We buy beautiful things, hoping they will help us calm our mind.

Mostly, I have waited for items to appear in my life. My meditation cushion is a pillow, shaped like a turtle, which my sister made for me a couple of years before I started meditating. My nephew bought me a shawl in Nepal.

In a sense, the paraphernalia hardly matters, because once we close our eyes, we are face to face with our own minds regardless of the outer regalia. We only need enough to be comfortable.

I do love watering my houseplants with the curly hose. And my purple shawl keeps me warm in the quiet hours of an early-morning meditation.

CUTTING TREES

To cut a tree down? Or not?

Living in the woods eventually has a drawback—shade (and all those tree roots) in the garden, and a shady (i.e., dark) house. We come to the forest for the trees, yet living in the shade, we yearn for sun.

A neighbor is having loggers cut down a swath of the pines that a farmer planted in 1939. The logging project began as a quest for more sunlight, since she recently had solar-voltaic panels installed. Now, the logging truck has made four trips to carry logs to the local sawmill.

We love our trees. The ones in our yard nearly acquire personalities. I've been parking my car under a hemlock for 20 years. I call it my Hemlock Garage, because of the protection it provides from snow and from sun. Who needs a garage with four walls when you have hemlock boughs overhead? Soon this hemlock will be cut down to make way for a real garage.

Like us, trees are of the nature to die—sometimes not of natural causes. We privilege our own viewpoint and our human needs.

And the tree says nothing.

SKUNK!

A skunk waddled across the road as we were driving home last night. Spring! The smell of skunk is the first sure sign of spring. The unpleasant smell gives rise to a pleasant thought.

We often want to push away the unpleasant. *No, thanks. I don't want any of that.*

But really, we can't hold on to anything. Neither the sighting of the first skunk nor its lingering odor. And not the thought of *Spring!* It's actually useless to push away or grasp for any thought, but that's what we spend our whole lives doing.

The skunk, the smell, the thought, the reading of this page is gone. Gone. Gone.

Leaving us with only this present moment.

photo credit: mirceax / iStock

THE JOY OF GIVING

I've gotten a whole month of blooms from those hyacinths in vases, but now they are nearly all gone. So, I turn my attention to the 25 pots of hyacinths and tulips that have been living in my garage since November. One by one I'm bringing them indoors, and one pot has begun to sprout.

You could say I am a flower locavore. Instead of buying cut flowers at a grocery store, I'm growing my own. And, I must say, these hyacinths and tulips are bringing me a lot of happiness. I even love to see them sprouting, before they have any flowers at all.

The Buddha tells us:

Giving brings happiness at every stage of its expression.
We experience joy in forming the intention to be generous,
we experience joy in the actual act of giving something,
and we experience joy in remembering the fact that we have given.

I have so enjoyed the intention—planting the bulbs and "hiding" them in the basement or garage makes me feel like a Secret Santa.

I also enjoy the intention of bringing them indoors and watching them sprout.

I definitely get a kick out of giving away the hyacinths, and, soon, the tulips.

And I do love the thought of all those spent hyacinth bulbs being planted in the ground in dozens of friends' gardens about a month from now.

Joy, joy, joy. I've got joy, joy, joy, joy down in my heart.

THE DELIGHT OF GIVING

My friend Trudy, aged 88, goes to the supermarket every Monday morning to pick up the flowers they are about to throw away as the fresh shipment arrives. She takes the flowers to the soup kitchen where she volunteers every Tuesday and Friday. She used to help make the salad or the main course, but new volunteers have taken over those responsibilities. Now her "job" is to arrange the flowers in vases for each table.

Trudy is also a painter of flowers, so many of these cast-off flowers show up in her daily watercolors. Sometimes she takes an arrangement of flowers to one of the two nearby nursing homes where she teaches painting once a week.

Generosity takes many forms. The supermarket is generous with its cast-off flowers. Trudy is generous with her time. Arranging flowers on the tables delights her.

What delights you about giving?

SWEEPING TEAK LEAVES

When I was on retreat in Thailand one February, the 4 P.M. chore was "sweeping" leaves. My rake looked more like a broom—a rather thin and ratty old broom, with just a few stalks of hard straw to do the "sweeping."

Our cottages were situated in a grove of young teak trees, which grow straight up quite fast. Teak leaves are larger than rhubarb leaves, and they are the consistency of a brown paper bag. February is the end of the dry season, so the slightest breeze brings more teak leaves drifting (crashing?) down to earth. Every morning, I awoke to find yesterday's clean sweep littered with more brown papery teak leaves.

Needless to say, I didn't look forward to this raking/sweeping chore. I tried picking up the gigantic leaves, but I quickly discovered red fire ants trooping along them, over my toes, and up my leg. I resumed sweeping.

After a few days, I realized that sweeping teak leaves is really what I do all day long in my everyday life. I straighten up the living room; next day, same thing. I clean up the kitchen; next day, same thing. I make the bed; next day....

Teak leaves keep falling in our lives. Leaves fall. We sweep them up. They decompose.

Just like our lives.

WHAT'S IN THE FRONT ROW?

It's time to start making space in my solarium for the spring plants. I'm potting up the rooted cuttings of many of my houseplants. I need more space, even though I've decided not to start seedlings (although it's not too late to change my mind).

So it's time to take the front-row plants and give them seats either in the balcony or the pit orchestra (i.e., my sweetie's music studio in the basement). Then I can push other, younger, more tender plants into the sunny front row.

What are some of our front-row re-actions? Impatience? Anxiety? Frustration? Worry? Planning? Yearning?

Can we take one of our bad habits and start working backwards, mindfully? Let's mindfully suppress the deed, the action. Then mindfully suppress the words on the tips of our tongues. Oh, this is hard work.

Let's mindfully feel the thoughts and emotions in our body. Oh, this is painful.

After several workouts of our mindfulness muscles over the course of a month or two, we will be surprised by the occasional arising of patience and kindness, concern and compassion.

Born out of concern for all beings, ourselves first of all.

BUYING THINGS AND GIVING THEM AWAY

While I was in Laos one February, I bought several silk scarves and Hmong coin purses, toiletry bags, and glasses cases. Shopping in the "night markets" of Vientiane and Luang Prabang, I felt that I was witnessing one big long display of eye-candy.

Now that I'm home, I put all the little silk tchotchkes in a basket and take them with me wherever I go. "Would you like a gift from Laos?" I ask my masseuse, my women's group, my writing group, my neighbors.

I enjoyed supporting the local Lao economy (by shopping), and now I'm enjoying passing those items along to women who will never travel to Laos.

Waking up at 3 this morning, I realize: *Oh, I buy things in order to give them away.*

This insight moves me down to my garden-book bookshelf, where I load up a box with beautiful garden-design books to give to my local library.

Oh! I see: I've decided to retire from designing gardens, a decision made without an "I" being involved at all.

It's just time to give away that beautiful clutter that I haven't really looked at for years.

TENDER SWEET FREESIA

Several years ago, I planted freesia bulbs in various large potted plants. Today I discovered a purple freesia blooming in the plumeria.

Freesia are *so* sweetly fragrant—I love their perfume. Yet, I really don't have the energy to focus on this tender bulb. I hid the freesia bulbs in houseplants so that they would surprise me—and they have been doing that for years.

Our tender qualities of heart are sometimes hidden behind a rough exterior or a thin veneer of niceness that we show to the world.

Let your kindness bloom today. What one thing can you do? What random act of kindness can you offer to your world? Without expecting anything in return. Without even expecting that people will like what you have done. Without even expecting that people will like **you**.

photo credit: altanakin / iStock

ROOT-BOUND

I just noticed that one pot of amaryllis has four good-sized bulbs in it, so I started to transplant them, each into its own individual pot.

When I turned the pot upside down, out fell another, smaller pot. The four bulbs bulged out of the small pot like a middle-aged woman trying to fit into a dress she wore as a teenager. Their growth had wedged them in so tightly that I could not shake them out, pull them out, nor push them out. A table knife eventually solved the problem: I cut around the edge as I would do for a cake stuck to a cake pan.

We can get so comfortable with our bad habits that we don't realize they don't fit any more. The cute sullenness of a teenager doesn't look so good on a middle-aged woman. Teenage lingo and speech patterns don't fit a young professional woman if she is serious about her career.

The first step in breaking a bad habit is simply to be mindful of it. Listen to it. Look at it. Feel it in your body. You don't have to change a thing. Simply by being mindful, you will have initiated a change.

GARDEN KARMA

In Native American traditions, March is sometimes called the month of the Starvation Moon. By this time of year, the summer's harvests are running low or have been completely devoured. Now, before the first green shoots and roots of spring, there is nothing to eat except the cambium layer of a few trees.

My own stores of last summer's harvest are thinning out. One pumpkin remains in the cellar. I still have about three dozen onions and a like number of garlic bulbs. The crisper drawer in the apartment-sized refrigerator in the basement is full of potatoes. But only one chili's worth of tomatillos remains.

Let me sing the praises of tomatillos—green tomato-like fruits in a paper husk—that are used in Mexican cooking. I picked them seven months ago, and now they are ripe and ready for cooking. Not unlike the fruits of our karma that ripen sometime in the future—sometimes sooner, sometimes later.

"You reap what you sow" applies not only to the fruits of our labors, but to our thoughts and actions, as well. Today, as we tend our inner and outer gardens, may we cultivate the seeds of kindness.

TOWN MEETING AND TOMATOES

Shall I start seedlings? Or not?

The first Tuesday in March is Town Meeting Day in Vermont. Two hundred or so of our town's 1,570 voters sit on metal chairs in the school gymnasium to decide, among other things, whether the town should spend $75,000 for a one-third share of a gravel pit. The Town Highway Department needs sand for winter's icy roads.

More importantly, Town Meeting Day is the day to start your tomato seeds.

I bow to tradition by at least looking at a bag of seed starter mix at the garden store. I wonder how my honey would feel about flats of six-packs on the dining room table.

What seeds would you like to plant and water in your inner garden? Kindness? Patience? Compassion for yourself? Generosity?

Choose one. Plant it today, and water it every day this week.

THE TOPOGRAPHY OF SNOW

"So, how's your garden?" people are asking me.

It's a joke. This morning the temperature is ten degrees—again. The flowerbeds are covered by two feet of snow so crusted with ice that snowshoes barely leave a track.

I'm starting to admire the topography of the snow, which is no longer smooth, but sculpted into hills and valleys as it melts. My yard looks like a relief map.

In other words, I'm desperate. The hyacinths I forced have finished blooming; my forced tulips have not yet begun to flower. I've given every houseplant a haircut, and I have 25 jars of cuttings sitting on a windowsill.

I would go into hibernation if I could, but the sun heats our passive-solar house, creating a tropical environment by 11 A.M. It's time to wake up and move. Squirrels scamper across the snow and devour the bird seed. New birds, more birds are showing up at the bird feeders every day—purple finches, flickers.

The earth is moving. The birds are moving. The snow is moving.

And so am I.

PROLIFERATING SPIDER PLANT

March is the time to clip all the "spiders" off my prolific spider plant and root them in a jar of water. They root very easily. In May, I will use the little plants as an edging in my white garden.

Yes, we usually think that a spider plant is a houseplant that belongs in a hanging basket, but why not plant it as an annual in the flowerbed? What fun to see an old friend in a new place! And all that edging is free.

As we become more familiar with joy, and how it naturally arises from a lack of desire, we find that joy proliferates, and we can "plant" it all over our life.

Time to take cuttings of the spider plant so it can proliferate.

photo credit: laurent rozier / iStock

STRESSED PLANTS AND STRESSFUL THOUGHTS

I have tomato plants growing in three different houseplants. I must have added compost to my potting soil last fall. The tomato plants themselves are winter-poor—pale green and leggy. Nevertheless, one of them has two ripe cherry tomatoes.

We know, theoretically, that stressed plants will bloom and fruit in order to reproduce before they die.

Our stressful mind states will also do just about anything to reproduce.

Recently, in a moment of open-hearted generosity, my sweetie offered a concert ticket to a friend. The next day he had second thoughts—and all of them were stressful. For instance, *She is such a free-loader* (Aversion) and *Hey, wait a minute! I want to go too.* (Desire.)

In order to reap the fruits (or cherry tomatoes) of the spiritual life, we have to keep an eye on our wholesome, non-stressful thoughts and actions. My sweetie acted generously. Generosity is a noble, an admirable, emotion. Let's grow more of that!

BULB SHOW

My women's group drove down to the Smith College Bulb Show for a blast of spring. Two greenhouses, filled with daffodils, tulips, and hyacinths, blooming apple trees and forsythia, and a multitude of other, smaller bulbs, transported us to May.

While we were there, we walked through the Palm House, the Succulent House, and the Orchid House. Oh, it was so hot and humid in there.

At home this morning the temperature was two degrees, and winter was still wearing her full regalia—two feet of snow, frozen in place.

Sometimes, we just need a reminder of the possible.

When your inner climate feels cold and dry, warm yourself up with gratitude and loving-kindness.

Write down three gratitudes right now.

I'm thankful for friends, flowers, and home-grown food. And I'm very grateful for you, dear reader.

IN THE PINK

"In the Pink" was the theme of a recent Smith College Bulb Show, with the centerpiece of the show being entirely pink.

The word "pink" comes from Dianthus, commonly called pinks. And they were called "pinks" due to their pinked edges (think: pinking shears).

We rarely use the verb "pinked," but the noun "pink" is part of our daily vocabulary.

Shakespeare used "pink" in the sense of "the best of," as "the pink of health" or "tickled pink."

The best qualities are the divine emotions, also called the Heavenly Houses or the Sublime States:

Loving-Kindness
Compassion
Appreciative Joy or Gladness
Equanimity

I've never thought of these Sublime States as pink before, but why not? They put us in the pink of mental health and happiness.

I was tickled pink to be at the Bulb Show with some of my best girlfriends. Tickled pink—another word for joyful.

LISIANTHUS FROM SEED

Susan is growing lisianthus from seed. These delicate flowers look like a Georgia O'Keefe painting, as layers of soft pastel petals unfurl. In the language of flowers, lisianthus symbolizes appreciation.

I myself have never succeeded in growing lisianthus.

I could envy Susan. I could envy her lisianthus. I could stamp my foot and say, "But I want lisianthus." Or I could appreciate her ability to grow them.

Envy is so much easier to feel than appreciation. It's not easy for our comparing minds to give the other person her due, to appreciate her skills and talents, to applaud her good fortune. Our comparing minds mistakenly believe in competition, that if we are not the winner, then we are the loser.

Susan is growing beautiful lisianthus. That has nothing to do with me; that says not the first thing about me.

I can simply appreciate her ability and her joy, and that gives rise to my own appreciative joy. After all, the message of lisianthus is appreciation.

GENEROUS WITH DAFFODILS

I recently gave a talk to the Valley Insight Meditation Society in Lebanon, New Hampshire. Doris, who sets up the room, drives more than an hour to sit with the sangha on the second Sunday of each month.

The group gathers in the lovely library of the AVA Gallery and Art Center, located in a former factory. Doris arranges the chairs and sets up a little side table with a statuette of a Buddha, a votive candle, and a small bouquet of flowers.

Both the candle and the flowers remind us of impermanence. The flame flickers, never the same flame, but never exactly different either. The daffodils remind us of the forthcoming spring and the impermanence of winter and the snow, which surrounds us.

At the end of the sit, when Doris extinguished the candle, she offered the daffodils to me. Oh, graceful generosity.

PLANTING SEEDS OF MINDFULNESS

I much prefer onion plants to onion sets. Onion sets are the tiny onions you can buy at the garden store anytime during the next couple of months. When I planted those, I was lucky to harvest onions the size of ping-pong balls.

One year, I started onions from seed. As a result, I harvested lots of tennis-ball-sized onions. After that I ordered onion plants for several years. This year I'm starting onion seeds again. I planted them in little trays on the day after the full moon.

According to *The Old Farmer's Almanac*, the seeds of below-ground crops should be started at the full moon to take advantage of the energy of the waning moon. Seeds of above-ground crops should be started in the dark of the moon (the new moon), so that the energy of the waxing moon will increase the growing energy of the seedlings.

The Biodynamic system of Rudolf Steiner is more complex, but I can't often organize my life on that day-by-day, moon-by-moon basis. I was just lucky to have the onion seeds, the seed starter mix, and the time to be able to start onion seeds at the new moon this week.

Sometimes we have to simplify our lives in order to plant ourselves on the meditation cushion. All we need is the cushion (or chair), a timer (cell phone or microwave), and the time.

Plant yourself today.

ABOUT TIME

It's about time, I suppose, to take the Christmas wreath off the front door. It's been looking a little peaked. The green circle of living balsam has lasted four months—from Christmas almost to Easter, from Hanukkah almost to Passover. There seems to be a certain poetic justice in that.

Yet it's just a story about time—as if time actually existed.

Time is just a way for the mind to compare past to present, past to future. In fact, past and future are mental constructions, with as much substance as a dream. The body, on the other hand, is always here now.

This gift of the present moment is the only place where we can be.

photo credit: oksix / iStock

FAITH IN MARCH

I received my first (and only?) Equinox card in the mail. Susan sends Equinox cards instead of Christmas cards. I like the idea. She included a poem by Celia Thaxter:

> *O March that blusters and March that blows,*
> *what color under your footsteps glows!*
> *Beauty you summon from winter snows,*
> *and you are the pathway that leads to the rose.*

The only color under my footsteps at the moment is white. The beauty that March summons is a matter of faith right now and for the next several days.

When I say "faith," I mean confidence or trust. Do we have the confidence that March will indeed summon beauty? Do we trust that March is the pathway leading to the rose?

Do we have the confidence that our meditation can lead us to moments of calm? Do we trust that mindfulness can make a dent in our infernal inner critic?

That's all the faith we need.

SEED STARTING

I went to the garden store yesterday for bags of seed-starting mix. Since I've reorganized my packets of seeds into little boxes labeled "March," "April," and "May," it seemed to be time to plant the March seeds indoors.

Which ones? Basil, of course. And tomatoes: grape tomatoes and my favorite Italian tomato, San Marzano. Do I really want to try eggplant again? I live in the woods in the North Country, and eggplants really need sun.

Let's get an early start on morning glories and zinnias. But why do I have Apricot Blush zinnias? That's not really "my" color.

When we sit down to meditate, we have many choices. What shall we cultivate today? Mindfulness of the breath? Mindfulness of the body via a body scan? Loving-kindness? Compassion for ourselves and for earthquake survivors?

The possibilities are many. Just for today, choose one. Plant that seed. And relax.

NO SNOW ON THE SEPTIC TANK!

A sure sign that spring is coming: The snow has melted off the septic tank! I haven't seen that piece of lawn since December, so even though it looks like frosty dead brown grass today, it's a welcome sight.

Those of you in the city rely on city sewer services, while those of us in the country rely on a big 1,000-gallon cement tank buried about eight feet under the lawn. The slight amount of heat generated by decomposing toilet waste and cooled shower water and dishwater is sufficient to warm the surrounding ground and thus melt the snow above.

To take advantage of this tiny March microclimate, I plant crocuses in the lawn above my septic tank.

The elements are in motion: snow (water element) is melting due to the heat (fire element) of the septic tank. The earth (earth element) plus water and warmth give rise to tiny crocuses wavering in the spring breeze (air element).

We, too, rely on earth, air, water, and heat for our own survival.

Welcome, Spring!

BARE GROUND ATTENTION

I can see bare ground out the back door! This may not sound like much to you, but I've felt stranded in my island of a house this month. Right now, my front yard is both ankle-deep in mud and knee-deep in snow. The septic tank melted yesterday—a neat rectangle in the snow. And now, finally, I can actually see part of my herb garden out the back door. Hallelujah!

Of course, I have to wade through thigh-deep snow, on the north side of the house, to get to the bare earth, and the dirt looks raw and un-beautiful. But I am overjoyed.

When we are meditating, we can sometimes dip under the cover of mind chatter, and simply pay bare attention to what's happening in the body, in the breath, and even in the mind. Bare attention means plain vanilla attention, with no judgments, no allergic reactions to unpleasant things, and no grasping for pleasant other things.

Just pay attention to the raw data of the senses. Pay attention to your life unfolding moment by moment.

Perhaps joy will quietly melt into you.

TIME TO DITCH THE CHRISTMAS TREE

Okay. Okay. Today I finally removed the Christmas wreath from the front door. That was easy. I took off the decorative pine cones and the bow, so I could re-use them when my women's group has its annual wreath-making party in early December.

But the Christmas tree.... Well, after I took those decorations off in January, I stuck the bare tree, still in its stand, in the snow in the front garden. It's rather nice to have an evergreen suddenly sprout full-grown near the front door. But then it got buried in a snowdrift, so that only the top ten inches of green peeked out. Now the top two feet have turned brown, while the bottom three feet remain under cover of snow and packed in ice.

Sometimes our bad habits are like this. We're ready to offload them. We can see the browning effect that smoking has on our lungs or that anger has on our nearest and dearest. Credit card debt singes our relationship with the other person whose name is on our checking account. But how the heck do we dislodge these habits?

Begin by practicing compassion for yourself. You might aim compassion straight at your own heart, or you might also include the hearts of your dear ones.

Place your hand on your heart. Right now. "Oh yes, my dear. I know you are suffering. May you rest in compassion."

SNOW ON DAFFODILS

Earlier this week, four inches of snow fell on daffodil shoots and tulip leaves that were peeking up through the mud.

"Oh no! What's going to happen to my daffodils?" a friend worried.

I could say, "Don't worry," but when has that ever stopped a worrywart? The crocuses and daffodils and hyacinths have it all worked out. They've been growing up through snow and mud for centuries. They don't say, "Oh, no!" They "know" to slow down when it's cold, and to take advantage of warm days to spread their foliage.

These late snows are called "poor man's fertilizer." Here's why: snow (like rain) captures nitrogen from the atmosphere and deposits it in the earth. Everything will be spring-greener as a result.

Sometimes our meditation is assailed by the five hindrances: desire; ill-will; anxiety/worry; sleepiness/lethargy; and doubt. Simply being mindful of these obstacles as they appear builds our meditation stamina. These dark clouds can fertilize our practice.

ROBINS REJOICE!

Robins are rejoicing this early morning, singing their "Cheer-up, Cheer-lee" ode to joy that bare ground has appeared. Let the worm feast begin!

In the same spirit, we too can perch for a moment in a comfortable chair with a nice view, perhaps with a cup of tea in hand, and express our gratitude that we have lived to see another day. Daylight is steaming ahead full throttle, warming our bodies making jackets superfluous.

We can count our blessings, not least of which is listening to the robins singing praises to spring.

photo credit: ThomasEricFoto / iStock

GARDEN WISDOM: 365 DAYS

TREE DETRITUS

These unseasonably warm March days spring me from the house. I feel like a tightly coiled noisemaker unfurled by the March wind.

What to do while the lawn is still soggy with snowmelt? I wrestle the garden cart out of the shed, where it's been stuffed all winter with other gardening paraphernalia. Of course, the cart's two tires are nearly flat from the long stretch of severe cold. I pump them up, so that, with the aid of the cart, I can become a beast of burden, hauling sticks to the brush pile.

Old Man Winter pruned more than the usual amount this year. Heavy pine boughs lie marooned at the edge of the driveway. Birch branches—both white and black—litter the lawn, the road, and my woodland walk.

In with the new season, out with the old exfoliated detritus of trees.

Welcome Spring!

ACKNOWLEDGMENTS

Our actions, our karma, ripple out to affect others in ways we cannot imagine.

Thank you, Michelle Taft, owner of Bayswater Books in Center Harbor, New Hampshire, for the offhand comment that I should write a 365-day book, thus setting this book in motion.

A deep bow of gratitude to Susan Pollack, who edited 965 blog entries from TheMeditativeGardener. blogspot.com down to a manageable 365.

Readers of my blog often tell me how one post or another has affected their lives or their thinking. Some are simply relieved to have a moment of mindfulness and a moment of inspiration while reading Facebook.

Thanks to you, dear reader. May our daily actions ripple out for the benefit of all living beings.

CPSIA information can be obtained
at www.ICGtesting.com
Printed in the USA
BVHW08s0517290618
520403BV00002B/2/P